# ROUTLEDGE LIBRARY EDITIONS: LOGIC

Volume 2

# NONDEDUCTIVE INFERENCE

# NONDEDUCTIVE INFERENCE

ROBERT ACKERMANN

LONDON AND NEW YORK

First published in 1966 by Routledge & Kegan Paul Ltd

This edition first published in 2020
by Routledge
2 Park Square, Milton Park, Abingdon, Oxon OX14 4RN

and by Routledge
52 Vanderbilt Avenue, New York, NY 10017

*Routledge is an imprint of the Taylor & Francis Group, an informa business*

© 1966 Robert Ackermann

All rights reserved. No part of this book may be reprinted or reproduced or utilised in any form or by any electronic, mechanical, or other means, now known or hereafter invented, including photocopying and recording, or in any information storage or retrieval system, without permission in writing from the publishers.

*Trademark notice*: Product or corporate names may be trademarks or registered trademarks, and are used only for identification and explanation without intent to infringe.

*British Library Cataloguing in Publication Data*
A catalogue record for this book is available from the British Library

ISBN: 978-0-367-41707-9 (Set)
ISBN: 978-0-367-81582-0 (Set) (ebk)
ISBN: 978-0-367-41746-8 (Volume 2) (hbk)
ISBN: 978-0-367-85390-7 (Volume 2) (ebk)

**Publisher's Note**
The publisher has gone to great lengths to ensure the quality of this reprint but points out that some imperfections in the original copies may be apparent.

**Disclaimer**
The publisher has made every effort to trace copyright holders and would welcome correspondence from those they have been unable to trace.

# NONDEDUCTIVE INFERENCE

BY

Robert Ackermann

LONDON: Routledge & Kegan Paul Ltd
NEW YORK: Dover Publications Inc

*First published 1966
in Great Britain by
Routledge & Kegan Paul Ltd
Broadway House, 68–74 Carter Lane
London, E.C.4
and in the USA by
Dover Publications Inc
180 Varick Street
New York, 10014*

*Copyright Robert Ackermann 1966*

*No part of this book may be reproduced
in any form without permission from
the publisher, except for the quotation
of brief passages in criticism*

*Printed in Great Britain
by Richard Clay (The Chaucer Press), Ltd
Bungay, Suffolk*

# CONTENTS

1 Inductive and Predictive Inference    *page* 1
2 Hypothesis and Predictive Inference    12
3 Probability and Predictive Inference    36
4 Statistical Inference    59
5 Bayesian Statistical Inference    83
6 Statistical Decision and Utility    104
7 Theories and Rationality    120
8 Bibliography    124
   Index    130

# Chapter One

# INDUCTIVE AND PREDICTIVE INFERENCE

The general problem of nondeductive inference is that of deciding what beliefs are reasonable when certain other beliefs are assumed to be true. In order to provide a basis for an objective study, it is usually supposed that beliefs can be represented by sentences to which a person would assent under appropriate conditions. Once this abstractive step is taken, deductive inference may be considered as a special case of the general problem of nondeductive inference. If someone assents to a sentence $A$ as expressing something that he believes to be true, and agrees at the same time that sentence $B$ is a deductive consequence of sentence $A$, then it only seems reasonable for him to assent also to sentence $B$. The interesting and crucial nondeductive cases occur when two people accept some sentences as expressing facts known to them both, but disagree on their interpretation, that is, on what hypotheses and predictions it is reasonable to believe on the basis of those facts. In such cases, deductive techniques are not sufficient to resolve the controversy, since hypotheses and predictions are never represented by sentences which can be *deduced* from the facts which are said to

## Inductive and Predictive Inference

justify them. Examples of hypotheses and predictions are sufficient to show that there is a problem of nondeductive inference without indicating whether or not that problem has a solution.

Suppose that two persons disagree about which of two hypotheses it is most reasonable to believe when certain facts are given. The hypotheses may be general statements, both of which explain the given facts satisfactorily, but which make different claims about some as yet unknown or unexamined states of affairs. This kind of nondeductive disagreement about which hypothesis is more reasonable can be looked upon as a controversy about whether or not there are more and less intelligent ways of tentatively extending human knowledge. Most of us feel that there are more and less intelligent ways: for example, that the use of scientific method is a more intelligent way of extending human knowledge than certain other methods; for example, trusting the pronouncements of soothsayers. The interesting problem given this assumption is to look for a characterization of scientific method that will be applicable to resolving disagreements between people who are attempting to follow scientific method, as it would be silly to contend that there are not serious arguments among scientists as to which hypotheses are best supported by certain available facts.

One solution to such disagreement is to simply allow each scientist to act upon whatever hypothesis he thinks best supported by the available facts. This solution very quickly runs into the difficulty that scientists do not act independently in that the experimentation of one may preclude the experimentation of another by irretrievably altering the subject of experimentation. If two scientists disagree about which method of

## Inductive and Predictive Inference

pest control would be most suitable in some ecological community and one of them is able to employ his method first, its failure may be accompanied by a change in the community so drastic that the other scientist's method cannot be tried. To speak of two scientists is partly metaphorical, since nondeductive problems often arise in an acute form for a single scientist who thinks that conflicting hypotheses are equally well supported by the available facts. It thus seems clear that a solution to the general problem of nondeductive inference, or solutions to particular problems of nondeductive inference, may be of considerable value in characterizing sound scientific method.

Contemporary logicians have made an attempt to look for solutions to the general problem of nondeductive inference by extending the techniques which have been successful in attacking problems of deductive inference. To consider these extensions, we may compare some examples of deductive problems with examples of nondeductive problems. At a relatively low level of abstraction, a problem of deductive inference is set whenever certain sentences are given as true and it is asked whether or not some other sentence can be the conclusion of a deductive argument whose premises are the given true sentences. The problem is solved if *valid* deductive rules can be cited whose correct use will permit the putative conclusion to be derived from the premises. A deductive rule is called *valid* in such a context if, and only if, its correct use never results in the derivation of a false conclusion from any set of true premises.

We can now set some frequently discussed nondeductive problems of a similar level of abstraction

## Inductive and Predictive Inference

and attempt to discover whether it is possible to find satisfactory nondeductive rules that will permit their solution. The first example of a nondeductive problem will be called the simple inductive problem. A *simple inductive problem* is set whenever two conflicting hypotheses are given along with some set of facts assumed to be true. It is assumed that the conflicting hypotheses are both compatible with the given facts. The problem is to decide whether one of the two hypotheses is more reasonable given the facts than is the other. A closely related nondeductive problem will be called the simple predictive problem. A *simple predictive problem* is set whenever some set of individuals has been examined to determine which of some set of properties each member of the set has, and two conflicting claims are made on the basis of this examination about which of the set of properties some as yet unexamined but otherwise identifiable individual (such as the next to be examined) will possess. The problem is to decide whether one of the two conflicting claims is more reasonable given the facts than is the other. For the most part, the discussion in this book will be restricted to a discussion of special cases of simple inductive problems and simple predictive problems, and it will centre about *rules* that have been proposed for making decisions which would solve these special cases.

Before examining these rules, it is useful to discuss some characteristics that such rules should be expected to possess. In comparison, proposed deductive rules must have the characteristic that their correct use can never lead from true premises to a false conclusion in some argument. Nondeductive rules for our special cases are used to choose which of two sentences (if either) it is *more reasonable* to believe when certain

## Inductive and Predictive Inference

sentences are assumed to be true. The more reasonable of two sentences given certain facts may well turn out to be false when further facts are made available, either because both sentences are false, or because the more reasonable may be false while the other is true because the facts given as the basis for making the original choice were misleading, i.e. poor ones for making the correct choice. If a true sentence is considered along with a false one on the basis of given facts, and a characteristic desired of a nondeductive rule is that it should always select the true sentence as the most reasonable, then the characteristic is identical with that for a deductive rule. But it is well known that no rule which tentatively *extends* human knowledge to make claims about unknown cases can lead *invariably* to true claims. The deductive characteristic is thus much too strong.

Consider again the claim that scientific method is superior to soothsaying. If we restrict ourselves to simple inductive and predictive problems, we might claim superiority for science on the grounds that a greater percentage of scientific choices in predictive and inductive problems have resulted in selection of a true sentence. *Success* in this sense may influence our view, but it cannot solve our problem. To begin with, we are not so much interested in relative success as we are in the reasons for relative success. For it is undoubtedly true, in the absence of statistical evidence to the contrary, that the percentage score of both scientists and soothsayers in selecting true statements as the result of nondeductive inferences is abysmally low. Surely very few of the hypotheses that may have been nondeductively inferred by scientists before 1800 are still considered to be *true* claims. We would not

## Inductive and Predictive Inference

switch from scientists to soothsayers merely because some soothsayer had made more successful predictions than any scientist over any period of time unless we found some reason to believe that the soothsayer's success was due to the use of a more reliable method. Our continued acceptance of scientific method as a reliable method in spite of its poor percentage success in finding true statements has led many philosophers to argue that the superiority of science is not due to decisively superior nondeductive techniques but to the technically superior vocabularies of scientists which result in the proposal of *quickly refutable conjectures* which shape a rapid sequence of rejected hypotheses that become harder to refute as time passes. (This point of view is developed in item [P2] of the Bibliography.) Pragmatists would argue against the criterion of success that no general test of the truth of a hypothesis is known. If this is so, no general measure of the relative success of scientists in simple inductive inferences can even in principle be adopted. According to this view, simple laws fitting the data in a given domain investigated by fixed instruments may always be disconfirmed when more precise instruments are invented. No hypothesis adopted as a result of inductive inference will ever be absolutely true because of this continual advance of experimentation. Yet pragmatists may nevertheless accept simple inductive inference as useful in choosing the most reasonable hypothesis to project at any given moment in scientific history.

If for these reasons no general test of success in inductive inference is possible, relative success in those cases where a true sentence is known to be one of the hypotheses or predictions given in a problem can still be an important partial criterion for nondeductive

## Inductive and Predictive Inference

rules. We could fill one urn with twenty white balls and another indistinguishable from it with ten white balls and ten black balls. An assistant may then shake up the urns and set them out in some order unknown to us. The problem of deciding which urn is which on the basis of a modest number of balls drawn from the urns would be a simple inductive problem. Now we would reject any inductive rule that would allow us to choose an urn from which we had drawn a black ball as the urn containing only white balls. This follows from the fact that the hypothesis is deductively incompatible with the evidence. Now let one urn be filled with ten white balls and ten black balls, and the other urn filled with eighteen white balls and two black balls. Then suppose that three white balls and two black balls drawn out of one urn and five white balls drawn out of the other urn constitute the facts on which we are to identify the urns. It seems intuitively reasonable that the urn from which three white balls and two black balls have been drawn should be taken as the urn whose contents are ten white and ten black balls by any reasonable nondeductive rule, even though it is logically possible that we could find that we had made a mistake by emptying the two urns. Although relative success cannot be a general criterion because there is not always a way of determining success in inductive and predictive inference, we do expect that sound nondeductive rules should conform to our intuitive expectations of relative success in simple examples where the possible alternative hypotheses can be specified and exhaustively tested.

In addition to success in simple cases where success is determinable, we should expect a nondeductive rule to be sensitive to the nature of the facts given in any

## Inductive and Predictive Inference

nondeductive problem to which it is applied. A rule for extending knowledge intelligently should presumably do so on the basis of the nature of the evidence which is at hand by comparison to the evidence which *would have been* at hand if the universe were different than it is. Thus, if all the balls drawn from some urn are black, it may seem a reasonable prediction in various circumstances that the next ball will also be black. This prediction could be supported by the putative nondeductive rule that if one is making a prediction about the colour of an as yet unexamined object, he should always predict that it will be black. But this rule would cause us to predict the next ball to be black even if all the balls drawn from the urn had been white, and this may be unreasonable in the circumstances. A rule which leaves the known facts out of account in deciding what is reasonable given those facts can hardly be a sound method of extending human knowledge. We may call the expectation that a nondeductive rule should support a hypothesis or prediction because of the evidence that has been accumulated by contrast to the evidence which might have been accumulated but was not accumulated the characteristic or criterion of sensitivity to evidence. It is this criterion which may chiefly distinguish deductive and nondeductive problems. In a deductive problem, we need only consider the given premises. In a nondeductive problem, we consider the evidence taken as true and contrast it to the evidence that might have been at hand if the facts were different in order to make a prediction or choose a hypothesis from some set of alternatives.

If a rule is to provide a solution to nondeductive conflict, we should also expect that it will produce an objective choice, that is, that two scientists using it in

## Inductive and Predictive Inference

connection with some simple inductive or predictive problem will choose the same hypothesis or the same prediction (if any can be chosen) on the basis of the evidence given in the problem. Some generalization of this feature would be expected for more difficult nondeductive problems, and we call generalizations of this expectation criteria of objectivity.

Summarizing, we expect a suitable nondeductive rule to yield a satisfactory intuitive expectation of success in simple examples, to be sensitive to the nature of the evidence given in any application of the rule, and to be objective in that it will lead unambiguously to the same solution of a nondeductive problem for different scientists accepting the same evidence. These criteria seem to be necessary conditions of any good nondeductive rule, but there is no proof that a rule satisfying them may not be otherwise unacceptable. It has proved extremely difficult as a first step in obtaining theories of nondeductive inference, however, to find nondeductive rules for special cases of nondeductive inference that will satisfy even these necessary conditions.

All of the proposed nondeductive rules that are to be considered in this monograph have a common feature: they locate a regularity in the facts given in the problem, or they see the facts as an instance of a hypothetical regularity, and the rule uses this regularity to *project* facts (often by deductive inference from a statement of the regularity) that enable the choice between hypotheses or predictions to be made. We shall call this general feature of the nondeductive rules proposed the *projection of regularity*.

A famous dispute in philosophy has been concerned with the question of whether or not the projection of

## Inductive and Predictive Inference

regularity is a legitimate way to base expectations of the future. This dispute has often been called the 'problem of the justification of induction'. Many philosophers have contended that the discovery of nondeductive rules having the criteria discussed above is of no value unless some reason or justification for expecting their use to be more intelligent than sheer guessing can be provided. This reason or justification is often thought to consist of an implicit or explicit postulate for scientific method which may be called 'the uniformity of nature'. In other words, this argument contends that the use of nondeductive rules which project regularities can only be justified on the assumption that at least some past observed regularities will continue to be observed regularities in the future.

The counter-argument to the claim that some such assumption must be made to justify nondeductive inference by rules is that the adoption of a postulate of uniformity does not help to resolve anything, since it cannot be known to be true. And if it is taken as a metaphysical postulate, it seems like a very circular kind of justification. If past projections of regularities suddenly begin to go wrong, nondeductive rules satisfying the criteria suggested above will begin to select regularities other than the ones which have failed as a means of choosing between hypotheses and predictions in new nondeductive problems. In this sense, nondeductive rules do not need any presupposition of uniformity since they can continue to be applied regardless of what previously projected regularities are found to have counter-examples. This line of approach suggests that the rules are not so much designed to single out regularities which are intrinsic features of the universe as they are designed to systematize the

## Inductive and Predictive Inference

choice of regularities that we use to try predictive extensions of in making nondeductive inferences. And the extension of regularity would seem to be the only way any prediction could be justified, for if the past exhibited no regularities, we could not perceive a pattern that we could recognize again as confirmation or disconfirmation of a hypothesis, and hence it would not be reasonable to extend human knowledge in one way rather than another so long as the alternative extensions were both compatible with the evidence.

### Further Reading

This monograph is intended to introduce the range of studies in nondeductive inference to the student who has acquired some competence in formal deductive logic, and who has been briefly introduced to the theorems of set theory and probability theory. At the end of each chapter, some references will be given to more complete or more advanced treatments of topics covered in the chapter. The bibliographies of these references must be used, in turn, to complete any reasonably full search of the important literature. Full references are given in the Bibliography. Occasionally, Greek letters are used in the text to correspond to those generally used for certain parameters in the literature. These are $\zeta$ (zeta), $\lambda$ (lambda), $\mu$ (mu), $\sigma$ (sigma), and $\tau$ (tau).

Issues connected with the justification of induction mentioned in Chapter One may be explored in [B6], Chapter VIII; [B8]; [G3], pp. 63–83; [K2]; [P2]; [R3]; [S6], pp. 228–236; and [W3]. [K2] contains a particularly comprehensive bibliography.

## Chapter Two

# HYPOTHESIS AND PREDICTIVE INFERENCE

Suppose two scientists watch a machine throw coins on to a surface, each throw of the machine resulting in three coins landing heads or tails. After thirty throws of the machine, one scientist records that 90 coins were observed, 45 landing heads and 45 landing tails. He adopts the hypothesis that the probability of any coin landing heads on the next toss of the machine is 1/2. The other scientist records that the thirty throws of the machine were such that every other throw starting with the first produced 2 heads and 1 tail, while the other throws produced 2 tails and 1 head. He adopts the hypothesis that the probability of any coin landing heads on the next toss of the machine is 2/3. These conflicting hypotheses are each projected from facts, but it is quite clear that the evidence for each scientist is different from the evidence for the other. The difficulty in comparing their evidence is that the evidence of each is about different individuals (single coins in one case, groups of three coins in the other) and they record different properties of *order* in the machine's production. No one has proposed satisfactory nondeductive rules for solving simple inductive

## *Hypothesis and Predictive Inference*

problems in which two conflicting hypotheses are based on differing evidence about the individuals which have been observed and the significance of the order in which they were observed.

The examples to be considered in this chapter are all examples of simple inductive inference or simple predictive inference in which the facts relevant to choosing between the hypotheses or predictions are observations of $n$ individuals such that each observation of one of the $n$ individuals results in attributing or not attributing some property to that individual. It will also be assumed that the *order* of observation is irrelevant, so that the facts can be represented by a *conjunction* of sentences reporting the results of the individual observations, a conjunction whose significance for nondeductive inference does not change when its conjunctive elements are rearranged.

Let the $n$ individuals examined in some body of fact be such that *all* of them have some property $P$ and no individual is known which does not have the property $P$. Then the principle of projecting regularities is compatible with adopting the hypothesis that all individuals (or at least all individuals like the examined individuals in some respect) have the property $P$, and also with predicting on the basis of this regularity that the next individual to be examined will also have the property $P$. This observation has been turned into a nondeductive rule of inference accepted by many logicians, and such a rule would seem to have the properties considered in the last chapter. The difficulty with hypotheses and predictions based on universally generalizing the occurrence of some property is that it is not obvious that there are any universal properties (properties possessed by all individuals) which are

## Hypothesis and Predictive Inference

useful in extending scientific knowledge, and it is not clear how simple inductive and predictive problems could arise on the basis of facts which would lead to but a single obvious generalization.

To take an example, if $n$ emeralds are observed to be green, and no non-green emeralds have been observed, then scientists may feel justified in positing the hypothesis that all emeralds are green, and they would no doubt expect that the next observed emerald would be green also. Actually, these projections would be based on more information than the simple reported facts about the colour of the observed emeralds, since scientists would no doubt have accepted other hypotheses which would suggest these posits, for example, the hypothesis that all the instances of a kind of gem usually possess similar coloration. If such supporting hypotheses are not available, the scientist might be more *cautious* in projecting properties seen to belong to all of the individuals which he has examined, but such a projection would sooner or later be in order if he continued to observe the same property in all of the emeralds that he examined. A scientist would not project the hypothesis 'Everything is a green emerald' but the hypothesis 'All emeralds are green', since noticing that each emerald is green is locating a regularity among emeralds only. To project a regularity *simpliciter* one could notice that this is equivalent to saying that everything is either not an emerald or it is green, i.e. that nothing is a non-green emerald.

Let $n$ individuals be observed to have or lack certain properties, this finding being reported in a conjunctive sentence which will be formally called the *evidence*. The evidence may *suggest* some *complex* property which may be consistently attributed to every indivi-

## Hypothesis and Predictive Inference

dual by projection. Let the projected generalization be called initially acceptable if the property which it attributes to every individual is such that it may be attributed to all of the individuals that are mentioned in the evidence, and no individual is known (informally, outside of those mentioned in the evidence) which lacks the property. We can call the view that generalizations may be usefully projected in this manner the *generalization principle*.

This form of the generalization principle removes the objection that there are no universal properties useful in extending scientific knowledge. The objection seems to rest on the notion that there are no intuitively simple properties that can be useful in this way, but the nondeductive rule allows us to project properties like 'not being an emerald or being green' which are of any intuitive degree of complexity relative to the language in which they are expressed. Indeed, most philosophers of science hold that a scientific *law* is always expressed by a sentence which attributes some such complex property to everything in the universe.

These observations can be made succinctly by the use of predicate logic. Let $Ex$ stand for '$x$ is an emerald' and $Gx$ for '$x$ is green'. If the $n$ individuals that have been examined are all emeralds and are all green, and if $a, b, c, \ldots, n$ are used as names for these examined individuals, then the observational facts may be summarized by the conjunctive sentence '$Ea . Ga . Eb . Gb \ldots En . Gn$'. The property of not being an emerald or being green can be represented by the expression '$-Ex \lor Gx$'. Now '$Ea . Ga$' implies '$-Ea \lor Ga$' in predicate logic, '$Eb . Gb$' implies '$-Eb \lor Gb$', and so on for the other $n$ individuals. If no emerald which is not green is known, we may

15

## Hypothesis and Predictive Inference

project the generalization '$(\forall x)(-Ex \vee Gx)$' (All emeralds are green) by the generalization principle. '$(\forall x)(-Ex \vee Gx)$' is equivalent in predicate logic to '$(\forall x)\ (Ex \supset Gx)$' and to '$(\forall x)(-Gx \supset -Ex)$'. These formulae could be expressed in English as 'All emeralds are green' and 'No non-green object is an emerald', respectively. Because these three generalizations are logically equivalent, it seems natural to suppose that the facts reported about the $n$ green emeralds allow us to project any one of these three generalizations.

Now suppose that the $n$ examined objects had all been non-emeralds of any colour. The facts would then have been reported by a conjunctive sentence like '$-Ea \,.\, Ga \,.\, -Eb \,.\, -Gb \,.\, -Ec \,.\, -Gc \ldots -En \,.\, Gn$'. But each individual is now not an emerald, and hence the property of not being an emerald or being green is true of each of the $n$ individuals as before, and if no non-green emeralds are known, then the generalization 'All emeralds are green' can be projected on the basis of this evidence by the generalization principle. It does not seem intuitively satisfactory to project the generalization 'All emeralds are green' on the basis of facts in which no emerald is mentioned.

A grid notation is now introduced which can be easily augmented to represent the evidence and hypotheses in the kind of situation which has just been discussed. Let $Ex$ and $Gx$ be as before, and form the grid on page 17.

A name for any individual examined in the evidence can be placed in the appropriate cell of this grid to indicate its observed properties. The property '$-Ex \vee Gx$' which is projected by generalization is represented in the grid by the L-shaped area which

*Hypothesis and Predictive Inference*

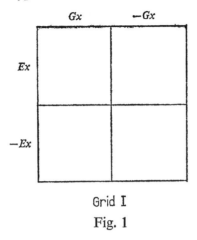

Grid I

Fig. 1

excludes only the upper right-hand cell. The generalization then says that everything has this property, i.e. that no object can be represented correctly as belonging to the upper right-hand cell. Thus the generalization can be represented by placing a null counter (Φ) in the upper right-hand cell of the grid to indicate that the generalization asserts this area to be empty. All of the logically equivalent hypotheses cited above are then represented by the same grid (see fig. 2).

Now *any* evidence which does *not* result in placing the name of some object in the upper right-hand cell of this grid suggests that any of the logically equivalent hypotheses represented by the grid could be projected. That is why evidence of green emeralds (names of such emeralds would go into the upper left-hand cell) is no more persuasive on this simple basis than evidence consisting exclusively of claims about non-emeralds, names for which would go into the two lower cells in the grid. A crucial difficulty for such projections is

17

*Hypothesis and Predictive Inference*

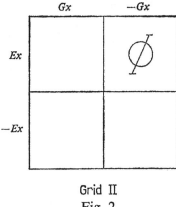

Grid II
Fig. 2

raised by the observation that if the evidence is only concerned with non-emeralds, and no emerald has been examined for colour at all, then *either* of the hypotheses 'No emeralds are green' or 'There are no emeralds' represented in the following grids

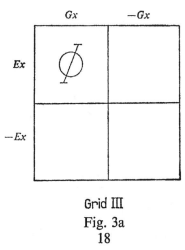

Grid III
Fig. 3a

*Hypothesis and Predictive Inference*

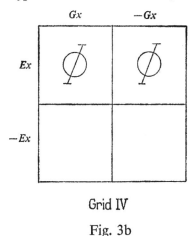

Grid IV

Fig. 3b

could be projected as well as the hypothesis 'All emeralds are green' by the generalization principle. This indicates a possible source of our dissatisfaction with projecting the generalization 'All emeralds are green' on the basis of an examination of non-emeralds only, since there is no more reason to project it than either of these two latter hypotheses.

A hypothesis will be said to be *compatible* with some evidence in a given grid if, and only if, the representation of the evidence in the grid does not result in placing a name into some cell of the grid in which the representation of the hypothesis places a null counter, otherwise it will be said to be *incompatible* with that evidence. The difficulty with evidence consisting entirely of non-emeralds is that it is compatible in the appropriate grid both with '$(\forall x)(Ex \supset Gx)$' and with '$(\forall x)(Ex \supset - Gx)$', whereas one might expect that evidence permitting *projection* of the former

## Hypothesis and Predictive Inference

hypothesis should prevent projection of the latter by being incompatible with it.

The possible hypotheses which may be expressed by placing a single null counter in a 2 × 2 grid may be related as pairs of contraries. Two hypotheses of the forms '$(\forall x)(\phi x \supset \phi x)$' and '$(\forall x)(\phi x \supset - \phi x)$' will be said to be a pair of contraries. '$(\forall x)(Ex \supset Gx)$' and '$(\forall x)(Ex \supset - Gx)$' are a pair of contraries, and so are '$(\forall x)(-Gx \supset - Ex)$' and '$(\forall x)(-Gx \supset Ex)$', a pair of negation signs being deleted in the last formula by predicate logic. A hypothesis which is a member of a pair of contrary hypotheses will be said to be *selectively confirmed* by evidence if, and only if, the representation of the evidence in a suitable grid is compatible with that hypothesis but not with its contrary. Let *a*, *b*, *c* be three individuals observed to be green emeralds, and let '$(\forall x)(Ex \supset Gx)$' and '$(\forall x)(Ex \supset - Gx)$' be the pair of contrary hypotheses. Grid V and Grid VI show that the evidence is compatible with '$(\forall x)(Ex \supset Gx)$' but incompatible with '$(\forall x)(Ex \supset - Gx)$'. This evidence hence

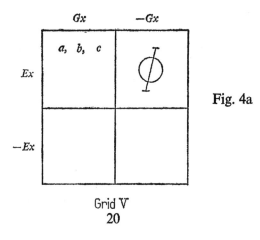

Fig. 4a

Grid V

*Hypothesis and Predictive Inference*

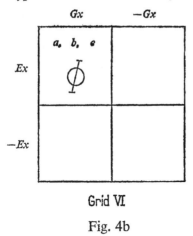

Fig. 4b

selectively confirms '$(\forall x)(Ex \supset Gx)$'. By constructing other grids, it is easily seen that evidence consisting only of the examination of non-emeralds does *not* selectively confirm '$(\forall x)(Ex \supset Gx)$'. This seems to be the desired result, and we may drop the simple generalization principle in favour of the rule that evidence will enable us to project any hypothesis that it selectively confirms, so long as no individual is known whose representation in a grid would be incompatible with the projected hypothesis.

The selective confirmation rule has some interesting consequences. Although the evidence represented in Grid V selectively confirms '$(\forall x)(Ex \supset Gx)$', it does not selectively confirm '$(\forall x)(-Gx \supset -Ex)$', although the two are equivalent by predicate logic. If logically equivalent hypotheses are taken as having the same informational content, '*A* is the contrary of *B*' is an intensional phrase, since one cannot conclude from

## Hypothesis and Predictive Inference

'$A$ is the contrary of $B$' and '$A$ and $C$ are logically equivalent' that '$C$ is the contrary of $B$'. This is reflected in the fact that logically equivalent hypotheses need not have logically equivalent contraries by the previous definition. To develop the notion of selective confirmation for a particular language seems to rest upon defining contrary hypotheses in terms of special syntactic features of the language. The result is that the notion of selective confirmation is not easy to generalize beyond hypotheses and evidence which may be appropriately represented in a $2 \times 2$ grid.

Our emerald example might arise in practice if a scientist were examining emeralds in order to extend knowledge about emeralds. In Grid V, only the evidence resulting from an examination of emeralds is represented, but this may be because the first row, in which all evidence about emeralds must be represented, is the focus of the scientist's attention. He might draw up the $2 \times 2$ grid we have shown because $Gx$ is the only property he has noticed that is invariably associated with being an emerald. His attention, however, cannot be represented in the grid, except by special convention, since the properties represented there formally might be any properties whatsoever. In the actual case where $Ex$ is the focus of attention, the row $-Ex$ may not be filled in because the scientist considers it general knowledge that there are individuals which would be represented in the bottom row if names for them were to be placed into the grid. Evidence represented in the upper left-hand cell may permit projection of '$(\forall x)(Ex \supset Gx)$' by selective confirmation, but it may also permit projection of the logically equivalent '$(\forall x)(-Gx \supset -Ex)$' since the scientist knows (informally) that there are many indi-

## Hypothesis and Predictive Inference

viduals which if represented by name in the lower right-hand cell, would project '$(\forall x)(-Gx \supset -Ex)$' by selective confirmation.

In nondeductive inference, it is often necessary to take into account information that is not explicitly cited in the evidence. A requirement referring to informal evidence cannot be logically or pragmatically inadmissible as long as the informal evidence could be formally stated in the explicit evidence for a nondeductive problem. We therefore define *positive confirmation* as an extension of selective confirmation. Let $n$ properties be used to define a grid appropriate for representing certain evidence and alternative hypotheses. Let $\phi x$ be one of the $n$ properties. Two hypotheses will be said to be *contraries* with respect to the grid if, and only if, their conjunction implies either '$(\forall x)(\phi x)$' or '$(\forall x)(-\phi x)$' for one of the $n$ properties by predicate logic, but neither hypothesis alone implies either of these. Consequently, if two hypotheses are both represented on a grid with respect to which they are contraries, a null counter will be placed in every cell defined either by the occurrence of one of the $n$ properties defining the cell, or by its absence. We now define the positive confirmation of a hypothesis with respect to given evidence. If evidence is such that some hypothesis is compatible with it, but all of the contraries of that hypothesis are incompatible with the evidence or with known cases of individuals not formally part of the evidence, the hypothesis is said to be *positively confirmed* by the evidence. Any selectively confirmed hypothesis may thus be positively confirmed if additional evidence of the proper kind is available. Positive confirmation is similar to enthymematic deductive inference. Grid V shows the hypothesis

## Hypothesis and Predictive Inference

'$(\forall x)(Ex \supset Gx)$' to be positively confirmed if individuals can be cited whose names would go into the lower right-hand cell of the grid. A claim of positive confirmation can be objectively settled by the citation of individuals whose names would go into enough cells that the resultant evidence would be incompatible with every contrary of the hypothesis in the grid while remaining compatible with the hypothesis.

The simple generalization principle cannot solve simple inductive problems satisfactorily. Either of the two contrary hypotheses '$(\forall x)(Ex \supset Gx)$' and '$(\forall x)(Ex \supset - Gx)$' may be projected on evidence in which the property $Ex$ is not attributed to any individual, and hence the simple generalization principle does not satisfy the criterion of objectivity. It may now seem that the adoption of the selective confirmation rule or the positive confirmation rule may prevent simple inductive problems from arising altogether, since if two scientists ascribe the same properties to $n$ individuals in given evidence, and if necessary agree on the properties of some other individuals, they can objectively agree on the hypotheses which may be projected on the basis of this evidence. To see that neither of these rules can solve simple inductive problems of a slightly more complex nature, we consider cases in which $n$ individuals are examined by two scientists who ascribe *different* properties to them. On such a basis, they may each project hypotheses satisfying (say) the positive confirmation rule for their own evidence, and yet their hypotheses may entail conflicting predictions.

Let the two examinations of the $n$ individuals disclose in the one case that all of them have properties represented by the predicates $Ex$ and $Gx$, and in the

## Hypothesis and Predictive Inference

other case that all of them have properties represented by *Ex* and *Ox*. If the two scientists are called *A* and *B* respectively, their proposed generalizations might be represented as follows:

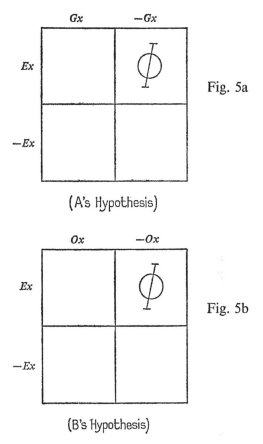

Fig. 5a

(A's Hypothesis)

Fig. 5b

(B's Hypothesis)

Now suppose that there is a property represented by *Tx* such that *A* can define *B*'s predicate *Ox* as

25

## Hypothesis and Predictive Inference

'$Tx \cdot Gx \vee -Tx \cdot -Gx$' and his predicate $-Ox$ as '$Tx \cdot -Gx \vee -Tx \cdot Gx$'. By adding the property represented by $Tx$ in defining his grid, he can represent both his hypothesis and $B$'s hypothesis on the same grid (shaded cells represent the occurrence of $Tx$):

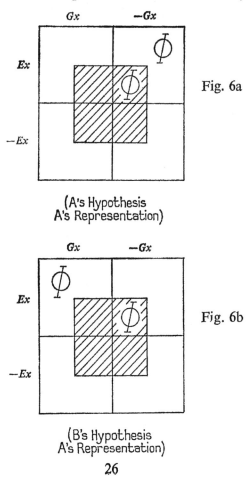

Fig. 6a

(A's Hypothesis
A's Representation)

Fig. 6b

(B's Hypothesis
A's Representation)

## Hypothesis and Predictive Inference

If the evidence attributes $Ex$, $Gx$, and $Tx$ to the $n$ individuals mentioned in it, it is easy to see that the evidence may positively confirm *both* $A$'s hypothesis and $B$'s hypothesis, so that both could be projected by the positive confirmation rule. Although the two hypotheses are compatible in that no contradiction can be deduced from them, they are predictively incompatible in the following sense. $A$'s hypothesis predicts that if an individual is found which has the properties represented by $Ex$ and $-Tx$, then it will also have the property represented by $Gx$, while $B$'s hypothesis predicts that under the same circumstances the object will not have the property represented by $Gx$. Thus if there is an individual with properties represented by $Ex$ and $-Tx$, the two hypotheses make contradictory claims, and as a consequence we should not want to project both.

From $A$'s standpoint, his representation of the two hypotheses may seem to favour his hypothesis, since $B$'s property $Ox$ is more complex than his property $Gx$, and his representation of the two hypotheses may seem to favour his in terms of conceptual simplicity. But the situation is exactly symmetrical for $B$. Using $-Tx$ and $Tx$, he can represent the two hypotheses on his own grids as shown on page 28.

There is little to choose from between $A$'s representations and $B$'s representations in terms of simplicity.

A very important example of this kind, from which it can be shown that this difficulty can arise for any evidence, is the example of *grue* emeralds introduced by Nelson Goodman. Let $Ex$ and $Gx$ be as before, and let $Tx$ stand for '$x$ is an examined individual'. Now by the previous definition given for $Ox$ in terms of $Gx$ and $Tx$, we could define a *grue* emerald as one which

*Hypothesis and Predictive Inference*

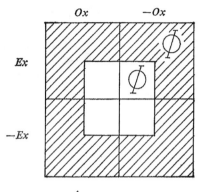

(B's Hypothesis
B's Representation)

Fig. 7

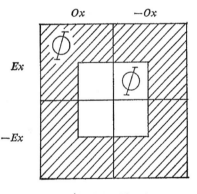

(A's Hypothesis
B's Representation)

Fig. 7a

was examined and green or not examined and some colour other than green. Then if all examined emeralds

## Hypothesis and Predictive Inference

were green, $A$'s projected hypothesis would be that every emerald was green, while $B$, attributing *grue* to the examined emeralds, would project the hypothesis that all emeralds were grue. These projections lead to conflicting predictions in that if another emerald is found, $A$'s hypothesis leads to the prediction that it will be green, while $B$'s hypothesis leads to the prediction that it will not be green. Intuition suggests that only $A$'s hypothesis should be projected while $B$'s should not, on the grounds that $B$'s hypothesis is somehow *ad hoc*.

Considerable attention has been given to the problem that *ad hoc* grue-like predicates can be constructed for any evidence class which will give rise to pairs of selectively and positively confirmed hypotheses from which incompatible predictions can be made. The problem illustrates the fact that the generalization principle, even in its revised selective and positive confirmation forms, cannot provide a suitable answer to simple inductive and predictive problems. Most attempts to advance on this impasse depend on supposing that the problem can be solved by ruling out one of the conflicting hypotheses on the grounds that at least one of the predicates used in its formulation is more *ad hoc* (grue-like) than any predicate used in the formulation of its rival. Attempts have been made to rule out grue-like predicates on the grounds that they are not *qualitative*, or on the grounds that they are not well entrenched.

It will not do to characterize qualitative predicates as those which may be used to formulate hypotheses which can be projected, since this procedure would be circular in an unhelpful way. Let *Ex* in the example be agreed to be qualitative. Green, for example, has been

## Hypothesis and Predictive Inference

distinguished as qualitative by comparison to grue by noting that grue's definition makes reference to a specific limited class of objects (the evidence class) while green does not, and by noting that any two green objects will always match a standard green patch while two grue objects will not always so match. This latter suggestion has been put as saying that green is an ostensive property because we can point to an example of green, while grue is not ostensive, since grue objects may not match, and so their exemplification would, at the very least, involve pointing to a variety of objects.

The objections to grue in terms of its reference to a specific limited class or to its inability to be defined ostensively can be seen to be language-dependent in an unfortunate way if a bit of science fiction may be introduced. Let *A* speak a *green* language in which *green* is defined ostensively by reference to a patch of standard colour. Let *B* (now a creature from an alien planet) speak a *grue* language in which *grue* is defined ostensively by reference to a patch of standard grue colour. This ostensive definition of *grue* for *B* must not be confused with the definition of *grue* in terms of examined emeralds given earlier. Suppose that *A* and *B* meet in space with standard colour patches and attempt intertranslation of their respective languages. Let *A*'s standard green patch match *B*'s standard grue patch to *A* and *B*'s mutual satisfaction. *A* may then conjecture that *B*'s *grue* is *green*, and *B* may conjecture that *A*'s *green* is *grue*. Suppose that *B* and his test patch are made up of grue matter which undergoes radioactive change at some moment after which *B* sees his standard patch as having the same colour, but *A* sees it as matching the standard colour patch that he calls *blue*. On the other hand, *B* now sees *A*'s green patch as matching the colour patch that he calls *bleen*. To *B*, *A* and his colour patch will have changed. *A* now revises his translation of *grue* to 'green until the change and blue thereafter', while *B* revises his translation of *green* to 'grue until the change, and bleen thereafter'. This situation is curiously symmetrical between *A* and *B*, since if it had been *A* and his colour patch that had undergone radioactive change, the translation revisions would have been exactly the same. In short, even if *A* and *B* were not parochial and wished to utilize that language in which *simple* terms correspond most closely to intrinsic properties of the universe, they might have no objective basis for choice. It would thus seem, in spite of the bizarre quality of this particular example, that there is no logical asymmetry between the way that grue and green might be used in different languages. This suggests that *absolutely qualitative* predicates cannot be distinguished by means of their role in a given language. For example, the fact that a predicate appears qualitative in one language because it is *primitive* (perhaps defined informally in an ostensive fashion) cannot be a proof that it is absolutely qualitative, since it may well occur as a non-primitive predicate in another language capable of expressing the same facts and hypotheses.

That this is of more than abstract interest can be seen from the possibility that a biologist and a sociologist, for example, may interpret given events in terms of different scientific vocabularies and consequently make incompatible predictions. Each may use a scientific language in which quite different primitives are taken as representing qualitative properties. But if the facts and hypotheses of each are translatable into

## Hypothesis and Predictive Inference

the facts and hypotheses of the other, or into facts and hypotheses which will make sense to the other, an argument about which regularity should be projected may issue in an argument as to whose primitives are really qualitative, and so far no solution has been found for this kind of argument that possesses the property of being objective. The rejoinder to this is often some form of the unified science hypothesis, to wit, that there is a privileged language of science (say the language of physics) whose primitives are truly qualitative and into which all other languages can be translated in so far as they are scientific. But even on such a hypothesis the development of science seems to indicate that there are no absolutely qualitative predicates to be used as primitives, since terms like *atom*, once taken as primitive, have received rather complex definitions in more contemporary physical theory. An attempt to avoid the difficulties in the notion of an absolutely qualitative predicate would therefore seem to rest upon some notion of qualitativeness with respect to a sound scientific language at the time of projection.

An attempt to avoid the difficulties with the notion of a qualitative property has been made by Nelson Goodman in terms of *entrenchment*. The entrenchment notion is that a choice between two properties that may be used in otherwise equivalent generalizations compatible with certain evidence (depending on whether the evidence is reported in terms of one predicate or the other) should be made on the basis of the number of times that the properties have been used in projected hypotheses in the past. This is perhaps tied to the intuitive notion of qualitativeness by the fact that properties which have been used in the past in successful projections are likely to receive a represen-

## Hypothesis and Predictive Inference

tation in language in terms of some short word. As entrenchment is defined in terms of the number of times that properties have been represented in past projected hypotheses, it avoids the apparent vagueness of the notion of a qualitative predicate. The number of times that a property has been represented (this includes its representation by different predicates) in projected hypotheses is at least in principle open to verification, and questions of relative entrenchment can often be settled to everyone's satisfaction without actually making a count.

Entrenchment will not solve every science fiction difficulty. If the *grue* and *green* speakers discover that *grue* and *green* are equally well entrenched in their respective languages, it may not be possible for them to decide that either of their hypotheses represents the more reasonable prediction. But within a language, it usually permits the solution of simple inductive and simple predictive problems. As English-speaking scientists we may accept 'All emeralds are green' and reject 'All emeralds are grue' where *grue* is given the definition in terms of examined cases, since *green* is clearly the better-entrenched property. Thus entrenchment at least points to rules satisfying the criterion of objectivity, along with the other criteria of the first chapter.

If we try to relate the entrenchment notion to the grids defined earlier, we might express it by saying that evidence should always be represented in grids whose cells are defined by properties that are more well entrenched than the properties used in defining alternative grids. This conservatism in choosing grids avoids the *ad hoc* quality of predicates like *grue*, since we are not allowed to use a new predicate on the entrenchment criterion unless no grid can be constructed out of predicates representing previously used properties that can represent the evidence and a compatible projectible hypothesis. In short, it rules out the construction of grids whose cells are arbitrarily fashioned to fit the evidence.

The entrenchment rules for choosing between arbitrary competing hypotheses in simple inductive problems of the kind discussed in this chapter are presented in considerable detail by Goodman (see [G3], pp. 94–117), along with some further choice criteria involving the background knowledge available at the time a projection is to be made. It has not been possible to show that these criteria are adequate, even in the sense that they will always result in a solution to simple inductive and simple predictive problems satisfying the criteria of the first chapter, but their improvement on the difficulties encountered by the criteria of selective and positive confirmation constitute a considerable advance on a general solution to simple inductive and simple predictive inference for the restricted kind of evidence that has been considered in this chapter.

## Further Reading

The difficulties with order of observation in simple inductive problems are succinctly stated in [C4]; [G4]; and [G6]. [S6], pp. 225–326, is a good introduction to the generalization principle and revisions of it leading to selective confirmation notions. This reference includes a useful bibliography on pp. 330–332. Goodman's notions of selective confirmation and entrenchment are fully discussed in [G3], pp. 63–126. Most of the contemporary work on the topics discussed in this

## Hypothesis and Predictive Inference

chapter is indebted to this very important and original discussion of projecting hypotheses. Other treatments of selective confirmation are found in [G1]; [L1]; [M1]; and [M4]. Difficulties with grue-like properties are analysed in [B1]; [G5]; [S1]; [S2]; and [U1].

## Chapter Three

# PROBABILITY AND PREDICTIVE INFERENCE

If the confirmation rules provided by the entrenchment notion are found to be satisfactory, there are still some questions that may be asked about simple inductive problems and simple predictive problems that such rules cannot answer. Suppose that the rules enable us to decide that one hypothesis is more reasonable than another hypothesis on given evidence. We may then wonder *how much more reasonable* the selected hypothesis is than the alternative, since if it is only slightly more reasonable we might prefer to accumulate more evidence before making a decision between them. There have been many attempts to solve the problem of measuring the reasonableness of hypotheses and predictions on given evidence by applying the mathematical theory of probability to the formulation of nondeductive problems. The intuitive idea is to proceed by expressing the statements involved in a fixed language, and then calculating the probabilities that the hypotheses or predictive statements are true when the statements contained in the evidence are assumed true. It is immediately obvious that even if such a procedure can be consistently car-

## Probability and Predictive Inference

ried out, its results will be closely related to the fixed language in which the nondeductive problem is formulated. Thus, if two people disagree about the appropriate language in which a nondeductive problem should be formulated, they may calculate different probabilities but their results will not be comparable in terms of these probabilities alone, since the probabilities will be functions of the language in which they are calculated. To apply probability notions to nondeductive problems, a preferred and definite language must be agreed upon in terms of which the problems are to be formulated. This amounts to saying that the philosophical difficulties uncovered in the last chapter must be assumed solved, so that nondeductive problems are being studied in a language whose predicates are at least in some sense aggregately more qualitative or more entrenched than the predicates of any known alternative language in which all of the features relevant to the solution of the problem may be expressed.

In this chapter we shall consider a detailed and impressive attempt to apply probability notions to the solution of simple inductive and simple predictive problems by Rudolf Carnap. Some knowledge of simple results of probability theory is required, and these results will be sketched here on the assumption that the reader is familiar with standard notation and simple theorems of set theory. These results will also be required in the following chapters on nondeductive statistical inference.

It is roughly true to say that the study of probability theory may be divided into a non-controversial formal system which is currently developed by mathematicians as a natural extension of certain functions

## *Probability and Predictive Inference*

studied in set theory and measure theory, and a controversial question of the circumstances under which this formal system may be used to extend human knowledge. In the following three chapters on statistical inference this latter controversial question will be discussed in more detail. Here we shall be content to see that Carnap's application satisfies the axioms of formal probability theory, and we shall be concerned with the intuitive feelings about such an application that Carnap's results either agree with or violate.

A conceptual physical device is described in order to illustrate the significance of the theorems of formal probability theory. Suppose that a very superior compass has its needle demagnetized and that it is then fastened down on some surface with a dial of 360° around the circumference of the needle's rotation that we are free to mark off into intervals in any way that we please. We shall also suppose that the needle and dial are so accurate that we can determine the exact point of the dial to which the needle points when it is at rest. We will further suppose that the bearing of the needle is so perfect that when the needle is spun sufficiently hard with a finger, it is as likely to stop on any given point of the dial as on any other. These last requirements cannot be met with exactitude in any physical instrument, but the instrument's working can be visualized with sufficient clarity to make it useful for illustrating probability theorems. In this use it will be called *the spinner*.

The axioms of formal probability theory represent conditions for the assignment of a probability function $P$ to certain kinds of collections of sets. In the general mathematical development probability functions are defined compatibly with these axioms on so-called

## Probability and Predictive Inference

Borel fields of sets. Applications of the theory, however, are usually in terms of probability functions defined on some set and the set of all of its subsets, and to simplify the discussion this will be the only case considered here. A probability function is defined as any function whose value for each subset of some set is compatible with three axioms to be given shortly. Students of formal logic should note that such a function may assign two distinct subsets the same value, so that it is not strictly a one-to-one relationship between the subsets and some set of real numbers. Although this violates criteria laid down by some formal logicians, the looser mathematical usage will be kept here. The theorems of formal probability theory develop the properties which any probability function $P$ satisfying the axioms of probability theory must possess.

Let $U$ be an arbitrary set. As the set of all subsets of $U$ is to be the range over which a probability function $P$ is defined, the various subsets of $U$ should represent all the possibilities whose probabilities of corresponding to some true state of affairs are to be compared. Because of this intuitive requirement, the set $U$ is called a *universe set*. In an application of the formal theory to problems concerning the spinner, for example, the various subsets of $U$ could represent the various ways in which the resting-point of the needle after a spin might be characterized. By an appropriate convention abstracting our intuitive reflections on the meaning of probability claims in simple cases, to say that a characterization of the needle's resting-place has probability 1 is to say that nothing could be more certain (given the problem of characterizing the needle's resting-place) than that that characterization of the resting-place will turn out to be correct, and to

## Probability and Predictive Inference

say that a characterization of the needle's resting-place has probability 0 is to say that nothing could be less certain than that that characterization of the resting-place will turn out to be correct. Probabilities of less than 0 or greater than 1 are not taken as meaningful. We thus expect that every subset of $U$ will have a probability of at least 0. Now suppose that the probabilities of two characterizations are known, and suppose that if one of these characterizations is true the other must be false. Again, by appeal to simple cases, we expect the probability that one *or* the other of the two characterizations will be correct to be the sum of their separate probabilities. Suppose that the probability that the spinner's needle will land in one interval of the dial is 1/8, and the probability that the spinner's needle will land in another interval which has no points in common with the first is 1/8, then the probability that the needle will land in one interval or the other will be $1/8 + 1/8 = 1/4$. Since the universe set is a characterization whose probability is at least as great as the probability of any of its subsets, we should expect that the characterization of the universe set is as correct as we can make it, i.e. that it has probability 1. These reflections, extended somewhat, lead to the three axioms of probability theory:

If $U$ is a set and $A_i$ an arbitrary subset of $U$, then $P(A_i)$ is a probability function defined on the set of all subsets of $U$ if, and only if:

(1) $P(A_i) \geq 0$,

(2) If $A_i (i = 1, 2, 3, \ldots)$ is a countable collection of pairwise disjoint subsets of $U$, then $P(A_1 \cup A_2 \cup A_3 \cup \ldots) = \sum_i P(A_i)$,

(3) $P(U) = 1$.

## Probability and Predictive Inference

The definition of a probability function satisfying these axioms for a specified universe set $U$ can be accomplished by specifying a collection of pairwise disjoint subsets of $U$ such that all of the subsets of $U$ can be defined as countable unions of members of this collection. Let us call any such collection of subsets of $U$ a collection or set of *simple subsets of U*, and designate any arbitrary simple subset of $U$ by $S_i$. A measure function $m(S_i)$ will be a function defined on a collection of simple subsets such that the probability function defined by the following definition will satisfy the axioms of formal probability theory for the universe set $U$ of which the $S_i$ are simple subsets.

*Definition* 1. If $A_i$ is a subset of $U$, and $S_j$ ($j = 1, 2, 3, \ldots$) a collection of simple subsets of $U$ which are pairwise disjoint such that $\bigcup_j S_j = A_i$, then $P(A_i) = \sum_j m(S_j)$.

It is trivial to find a collection of simple subsets and measure functions such that they lead by Definition 1 to probability functions where $U$ is a finite set. Let $U = \{u_1, u_2, \ldots, u_n\}$ be a finite universe set of $n$ elements. Let $S_i = \{u_i\}$ ($i = 1, 2, \ldots, n$) be a collection of $n$ simple subsets, each $S_i$ consisting of a set whose only element is a distinct element of $U$. Any function $m(S_i)$ such that $m(S_i) \geqslant 0$ (for all $i$) and $\sum_i S_i = 1$ defines by Definition 1 a probability function satisfying the axioms. Each subset of $U$ can be defined in terms of the elements of $U$ which are elements of the subset, and hence the subset is identical to some union of appropriate simple subsets and its probability function value may be calculated through the use of Definition 1. It is easy to show that the probability of the subset of $U$

containing no elements of $U$ is 0 in the formal development.

To take an example, let $u_1 = \{0° < x \leqslant 60°\}$ be that interval on the spinner's dial which consists of all points representing degrees greater than 0°, or less than or equal to 60°. Similarly define $u_2 = \{60° < x \leqslant 120°\}$, $u_3 = \{120° < x \leqslant 180°\}$, $u_4 = \{180° < x \leqslant 240°\}$, $u_5 = \{240° < x \leqslant 300°\}$, and $u_6 = \{300° < x \leqslant 360°\}$. The set $U = \{u_1, u_2, u_3, u_4, u_5, u_6\}$ is a finite set of six elements such that at least one of them and at most one of them can be a representation of the needle's position after it has been spun. Any set whose elements are such that exactly one of them will be the correct characterization of some state of affairs may be called a finite probability space. Other subsets of $U$ may represent other correct characterizations. If the needle stops on the point representing 78°, $u_2$ is a correct characterization of its position, but so is $\{u_2, u_3\}$ which is the characterization of the needle's position as being either in the second or the third interval. Now by the construction of the spinner, we expect $P\{u_1\} = P\{u_2\} = P\{u_3\} = P\{u_4\} = P\{u_5\} = P\{u_6\}$ for the probability function values of these equal intervals on the spinner's dial. Let $S_i = u_i$ ($i = 1, 2, \ldots, 6$) be the simple subsets of $U$, and define $m(S_i)$ as a measure function having the following values: $m(S_1) = m(S_2) = m(S_3) = m(S_4) = m(S_5) = m(S_6) = 1/6$. The three axioms of probability theory are satisfied when $P$ is defined on this particular $U$ using this measure function and Definition 1. For example, since $U = \bigcup_i (S_i)$, $P(U) = \sum_i m(S_i) = 1$, so that axiom (3) is satisfied.

So far we have discussed satisfaction of the axioms for finite universe sets only. Now let $U$ be an infinite

## Probability and Predictive Inference

universe set. The method of using a measure function to define the probability function values of sets containing but one element of $U$, and then utilizing Definition 1 to calculate other probability function values will not work in general for infinite sets. This can be shown through another example involving the spinner. Let $U$ in this example be the set of all of the points on which the needle may come to rest. By the properties of the spinner, the probability function value for every subset of $U$ consisting of only one such point must be equal to the probability function value for every other such subset. It is easy to show that this value must consequently be 0. Suppose $P(A_i) = e > 0$, where $A_i$ is any subset of $U$ containing only one element of $U$. Let $B$ be any subset of $U$ containing $e$ distinct points which are elements of $U$. By taking repeated unions of distinct $A_i$, and using axiom (2), $P(B) = 1$. Let $C$ be a subset of $U$ formed by taking the union of $B$ with some $A_i$ whose element is not an element of $B$. By axiom (2), $P(C) = 1 + e$, but as $C \subset U$, this contradicts axiom (3). Consequently, $P(A_i) \neq e > 0$. If the axioms can be satisfied for an infinite set $U$, therefore, $P(A_i) = 0$. Suppose a measure function whose values are $m(A_i) = 0$ for all $i$ to be defined. Definition 1 for the case of $U$ is now $P(U) = \sum_i m(A_i)$. But the sum on the right-hand side can never be greater than 0. If $U$ is infinite and $P(U)$ is given by Definition 1 and a measure function which only assigns the value 0 to elements of $U$, then axiom (3) will not be satisfied. There are many ways of explaining the difficulty. In the case of the spinner, the source of the problem is that there are more than a countable number of points on the spinner's dial, but any set of points the measure function values of which

## Probability and Predictive Inference

are summed by Definition 1 must be countable. To find suitable measure functions and probability functions defined on them which will satisfy the axioms of probability for the infinite case, it is often necessary to use techniques of mathematical analysis which are beyond the expected competence of the student of philosophy.

In the case of the spinner, however, it is possible to describe a probability function that will satisfy the axioms. We begin by considering *intervals* on the spinner's dial. An interval will be defined as a set consisting of *all* of the points *between* two specified points on the spinner's dial. The point representing 20° and the point representing 140° define the interval $\{20° < x < 140°\}$, but neither of these points belongs to the interval. If $\{a < x < b\}$ is an interval, we let $[a, b]$ be an alternative notation for the same interval. We define the measure-function value of any interval as the ratio of the *length* of that interval (the distance between the two points defining it) to the length of the entire dial (the interval $[0°, 360°]$), which is defined as having the length 1. Thus $m\{20° < x < 140°\} = m[20°, 140°] = 1/3$. If the two points defining an interval are identical, save for the interval $[0°, 360°]$, which is defined as having all the points of $U$ save one in it, then the interval is said to be a *degenerate interval*, and is defined as identical to the set consisting of the single point which defines its degenerate length. Thus $\{20° < x < 20°\} = [20°, 20°] = \{20°\}$. The length of any degenerate interval is 0. Thus, $m[20°, 20°] = m\{20°\} = 0$. We let the collection of all sets which are either intervals or degenerate intervals be the simple subsets of $U$, and let the measure function on these simple subsets have the values which have been indicated. $U$ is the set of all points on the spinner's dial. Any subset of $U$ can be defined as the union of non-overlapping intervals and degenerate intervals. $U$, for example, is the union of the interval $[0°, 360°]$ with the degenerate interval $[0°, 0°]$. $U$ may therefore be represented as $\{\{0° < x < 360°\}, \{0°\}\}$. Now $m\{0° < x < 360°\} = 1$ and $m\{0°\} = 0$ by the definition of the measure function. Axiom (3) is therefore satisfied by the probability function given by this measure function and Definition 1.

We now suppose that a $P$ satisfying the axioms has been defined by Definition 1 on the basis of a measure function over simple subsets of some set. Strictly speaking, axiom (2) defines only the union of pairwise disjoint sets. The theorems of probability theory establish identities between the probabilities of various sets by means of set theoretic and arithmetic operations. These theorems are not required to *find* the probability of any set. For example, let us consider the intersection $A_1 \frown A_2$ of two arbitrary subsets $A_1$ and $A_2$ of $U$. Since $A_1 \frown A_2$ will be a subset of $U$, we can build up the probability value $P(A_1 \frown A_2)$ by finding $A_1 \frown A_2$ as a union of simple subsets. But suppose that we have already calculated the value of $P(A_1 \frown A_2)$ in this way. We may be interested in the probability value of $A_1 \smile A_2$, the union of the two subsets $A_1$ and $A_2$. Since $A_1$ and $A_2$ may not be disjoint, axiom (2) does not provide a general solution. Now consider the following theorem:

Addition Theorem:

$P(A_1 \smile A_2) = P(A_1) + P(A_2) - P(A_1 \frown A_2).$

Let $A_1 - A_2$ be the set (possibly null) whose elements are those elements of $A_1$ which are not elements of $A_2$.

## Probability and Predictive Inference

Since $A_1 \cap A_2$ is the set whose elements are those elements of $A_1$ which are elements of $A_2$, we find from set theory that $(A_1 - A_2) \cap (A_1 \cap A_2) = \Phi$, and also that $A_1 = (A_1 - A_2) \cup (A_1 \cap A_2)$. Similarly,

$$(A_2 - A_1) \cap (A_1 \cap A_2) = \Phi$$

and

$$A_2 = (A_2 - A_1) \cup (A_1 \cap A_2).$$

$A_1 \cup A_2$ is the set whose elements are elements of $A_1$ and not $A_2$, or elements of $A_1$ and $A_2$, or elements of $A_2$ and not $A_1$. Consequently,

$$A_1 \cup A_2 = (A_1 - A_2) \cup (A_1 \cap A_2) \cup (A_2 - A_1).$$

Using axiom (2) and the fact that the three sets on the right-hand side are pairwise disjoint, we have

$$P(A_1) = P(A_1 - A_2) + P(A_1 \cap A_2)$$

and

$$P(A_2) = P(A_2 - A_1) + P(A_1 \cap A_2).$$

Further,

$$P((A_1 - A_2) \cup (A_2 - A_1) \cup (A_1 \cap A_2)) = P(A_1 - A_2) + P(A_2 - A_1) + P(A_1 \cap A_2)$$

by axiom (2). Substitution of the identities proved into the Addition Theorem reduces the latter to an obvious arithmetic identity, thus proving the Addition Theorem from set theoretic considerations. When certain probability function values are already known, theorems like the Addition Theorem facilitate the computation of probability function values for arbitrary subsets of $U$.

An example of the use of the Addition Theorem is easily given. Let $U$ be the universe set $\{u_1, u_2, u_3, u_4, u_5, u_6\}$ of six equal intervals on the spinner's dial given earlier. Let $A_1 = \{u_1, u_2\}$ and $A_2 = \{u_2, u_3\}$. It is easy

*Probability and Predictive Inference*

to calculate $P(A_1) = P(A_2) = 1/3$, and $P(A_1 \frown A_2) = P\{u_2\} = 1/6$ from Definition 1 and the measure function given earlier. Substituting these values in the Addition Theorem, we have $P(A_1 \smile A_2) = 1/3 + 1/3 - 1/6 = 1/2$, a result which is identical with that derived from direct calculation.

A definition of *conditional probability* is useful in developing further theorems. If we know that some element of $U$ is a member of a subset $A_1$, we may wonder what the probability is that that element is also an element of another subset $A_2$. This is expressed in the formal theory as $P(A_2 \mid A_1)$, the *conditional probability* that an element of $U$ which is an element of $A_1$ is also an element of $A_2$. It is defined by the following:

*Conditional Probability Definition,*

$$P(A_2 \mid A_1) = \frac{P(A_1 \frown A_2)}{P(A_1)}.$$

An example involving the spinner may make the significance of this clearer. Using the universe set $U$ whose elements are the six equal intervals, $P(\{u_1\} \mid \{u_1, u_2, u_3\})$ would represent the conditional probability of the needle's stopping in the first interval of the spinner's dial if it was known that it had stopped somewhere in the first three intervals. Substituting into the Conditional Probability Definition, this is $1/3$, in agreement with intuition. Notice that $P(\{u_1, u_2, u_3\} \mid \{u_1\}) = 1$ reflects the trivial fact that if the needle is known to have stopped in the first interval of the dial, it is also known to have stopped in one of the first three intervals of the dial.

We turn now to the representative attempt to use formal probability theory to solve simple inductive problems and predictive problems that has been made

## Probability and Predictive Inference

by Rudolf Carnap. To find an interpretation for the calculus of probability that will solve simple inductive and predictive problems, Carnap begins with an axiomatized language $L$ in which the evidence cited in such a problem by scientists may be adequately described. Such a fixed language $L$ is used to define a degree of confirmation function $c(h, e)$ which assigns a real number between 0 and 1 as a measure of the degree of reasonableness of the sentence $h$ of the language $L$ when sentence $e$ summarizes the total available evidence as it is described in $L$. Two conditions are placed on $L$. First, its variables are taken to range over an infinite number of individuals. Secondly, its extralogical primitive terms must be arranged in groups of *families* of predicates. A group of predicates is a *family of predicates* in $L$ if, and only if, any individual in the range of the quantifiers of $L$ must necessarily be denoted by one, and only one, of the predicates. The pair of predicates '$x$ is blue' and '$x$ is non-blue' constitute a family since any individual must either be blue or non-blue. No predicate can belong to more than one family of $L$. In a language $L$ for scientific evidence this primitive family would be embedded in a family of predicates representing every possible observable colour.

The significance of the way in which $c(h, e)$ is defined can be illustrated by considering how $c(h, e)$ might be defined (and *was* defined in Carnap's early works) in a language $L'$ which has the same predicates as a language $L$, but whose quantifiers range only over a finite number of individuals. In order to discuss this briefly, we will take a language $L^*$ of this kind whose only family of predicates is $Bx$ and $-Bx$, and whose quantifiers range over three individuals $a$, $b$, and $c$.

## Probability and Predictive Inference

Now *if* the universe only contained these three individuals, and the only properties we could distinguish by means of language $L^*$ were $Bx$ and $-Bx$, then language $L^*$ could describe only eight *possible* worlds, one of which would have to be the world that we live in, although there might be more to say about our world than $L^*$ permits us to say. Each of these possible worlds is described in $L^*$ by a conjunction of three sentences, each of which says whether or not one of the individuals $a$, $b$, or $c$ has the property represented by $Bx$ in that world. The possible worlds that can be described in $L^*$ are thus:

| | |
|---|---|
| $Ba . Bb . Bc$ | ($w1$) |
| $Ba . Bb . -Bc$ | ($w2$) |
| $Ba . -Bb . Bc$ | ($w3$) |
| $Ba . -Bb . -Bc$ | ($w4$) |
| $-Ba . Bb . Bc$ | ($w5$) |
| $-Ba . Bb . -Bc$ | ($w6$) |
| $-Ba . -Bb . Bc$ | ($w7$) |
| $-Ba . -Bb . -Bc$ | ($w8$) |

The universe set $U$ (for the purpose of interpreting the formal theory of probability in $L^*$) has as its elements these eight possible worlds. Now any assertion that can be made in $L^*$ about the world is equivalent to asserting that the world we live in is represented by some subset of $U$. Thus, $(\forall x)(Bx)$, which asserts that everything has the property represented by $Bx$, is equivalent to asserting that the world we live in is correctly described by the subset $\{Ba . Bb . Bc\}$. The assertion that 2/3 of all individuals are denoted by $Bx$ is equivalent to asserting that the world we live in is described by the set $\{Ba . Bb . -Bc, Ba . -Bb . Bc,$

## *Probability and Predictive Inference*

—$Ba \cdot Bb \cdot Bc\}$. Notice that we are either not permitted to say that 1/4 of all individuals are denoted by $Bx$ in $L^*$, or we conclude that this assertion is the same as the assertion that 3/4 of all individuals are denoted by $Bx$ in $L^*$, since both of these claims, if representable at all, must be represented by the null subset of $U$. It is the extension of this difficulty to various statistical claims in any universe of finite size that accounts, among other reasons, for the fact that $c(h, e)$ is only defined in Carnap's current systems in languages $L$ whose quantifiers range over an infinite number of individuals.

Any evidence claim and any hypothesis in $L^*$ (or a language $L$) can be represented by subsets of $U$. The conjunction of any hypothesis and evidence statement is also a statement which may be represented by the subset of $U$ consisting of all of the elements of $U$ which describe worlds in which the statement would be true. The *degree of confirmation* (the value of $c(h, e)$) of $h$ given $e$ is then defined as a probability function by

$$\frac{P\{h \cdot e\}}{P\{e\}},$$

where $P$ is a probability function defined by Definition 1 in terms of a finite measure function on subsets of $U$ containing only one element of $U$. $\{h \cdot e\}$ stands for the subset of $U$ representing the claim made by the statement $h \cdot e$. The intuitive idea is strikingly clear, as the degree of confirmation of a statement $h$ on the basis of a statement $e$ is formally the conditional probability of $h$ given $e$ in $U$, and is represented in Carnap's interpretation as the ratio of the probability of the subset of $U$ describing the possible worlds in which the conjunction of $h$ and $e$ would be true to the probability of

## Probability and Predictive Inference

the subset of $U$ describing the possible worlds in which $e$ would be true. Since we expect evidence to assert something about the world, and since we expect a hypothesis compatible with the evidence to assert what the evidence asserts as well as something in addition, this ratio should always be well-defined and it should have the formal properties of a conditional probability value, at least in a language like $L^*$, where the possible worlds that can be described in $L^*$ can be taken as the elements of a finite probability space. The probability function $P$ is defined for the set of all possible subsets of the set whose elements are the possible worlds which may be described in the language, and the value of $c(h, e)$ is then calculated from $P$ by the given formula.

Suppose that there are $n$ possible worlds represented as elements of $U$. One possible measure function $m$ for defining a probability function is that which assigns equal weight to every element of $U$. A typically interesting result of Carnap's investigation of $c(h, e)$ functions is that a $c(h, e)$ function defined on a measure function assigning equal weight to every element of $U$ violates the criterion of nondeductive rules that they should be sensitive to the facts described by the evidence. Let $e$ be the evidence statement $Ba . Bb$ expressed in $L^*$. Let $h$ be $Bc$. We wish to calculate $c(h, e)$ for this $h$ and $e$, that is, the probability that $c$ will be denoted by $Bx$ when $a$ and $b$ have been. $(h . e)$ is equivalent to $\{Ba . Bb . Bc\}$, but this has as its only element one of the eight elements of $U$, i.e. $w1$, and would be assigned the probability function value $1/8$ in $L^*$ by a measure function assigning equal weights to the elements of $U$. $e$ is $Ba . Bb$, but this assertion is true in the two possible worlds $w_1$ and $w_2$

## Probability and Predictive Inference

and in no others, so $e$ is represented by the subset $\{w_1, w_2\}$. If the measure function assigns equal values to each simple subset $\{w_i\}$ ($i = 1, 2, \ldots, 8$), then $m\{w_1\} = m\{w_2\} = 1/8$, so by Definition 1 $P\{w_1, w_2\} = 2/8$. Consequently, $c(h, e) = P(h . e)/P(e) = 1/8 // 2/8 = 1/2$. Suppose the evidence had been the assertion $e'$ or $Ba . -Bb$ instead. By similar calculations, $c(h, e') = 1/2$, and even if the evidence had been $e''$ or $-Ba . -Bb$, $c(h, e'')$ would also have the value $1/2$. The result of taking the measure function $m$ which assigns equal weight to every element of $U$ thus has the result that any observation of individuals being or not being denoted by $Bx$ results in the probability $1/2$ of the next individual being denoted by $Bx$. Thus the measure function leads to a probability function which is *a priori*, that is, one whose solution of simple inductive and simple predictive problems is independent of the nature of the evidence given in the problem.

Among the many possible alternative logically consistent functions, Carnap selects a measure function $m^*$ as leading to the most intuitively satisfactory values for a degree of confirmation function. The measure function $m^*$ results in the assignment of equal probability function values to every *structure* in a language like $L^*$. A *structure* in $L^*$ is a description of the world which characterizes the world in terms of what number of or ratio of individuals have or do not have certain predicates from the various families of predicates. In $L^*$, there are only four structures. These are the worlds in which all three individuals are denoted by $Bx$, the worlds in which two individuals only are denoted by $Bx$, the worlds in which one individual only is denoted by $Bx$, and the worlds in which no individuals are denoted by $Bx$. Let us call these four structures $STR_3$, $STR_2$, $STR_1$, and $STR_0$, respectively. Of the eight possible worlds $w_1, w_2, \ldots, w_8$ which may be described in $L^*$, $w_1$ belongs to $STR_3$, $w_2$, $w_3$, and $w_5$ belong to $STR_2$, $w_4$, $w_6$, and $w_7$ belong to $STR_1$, and $w_8$ belongs to $STR_0$. $m^*$ assigns equal values (1/4 in $L^*$) to each structure of a language. If a structure has more than one element of $U$ belonging to it, the $m^*$ value given to the structure is divided equally among these elements. If $\tau$ is the number of structures in a language like $L^*$, and $\zeta_i$ is the number of elements of $U$ in the same structure as an element $u_i$ of $U$, then

$$m^*(u_i) = 1/\tau\zeta_i.$$

Using this measure function along with Definition 1, we derive the confirmation function $c^*(h, e)$:

$$c^*(h, e) = \frac{P\{h \cdot e\}}{P\{e\}}.$$

This is Carnap's proposal for a degree of confirmation function in finite languages.

$c^*(h, e)$ leads to more reasonable values than $c(h, e)$ in the case considered earlier. If $h, e, e', e''$ are as above, we expect that the degree of confirmation value of $h$ on evidence $e$ should be higher than the value of $h$ on $e'$, and that this should be higher than the value of $h$ on $e''$, i.e.:

$$c^*(h, e) > c^*(h, e') > c^*(h, e'').$$

Calculation shows that this ordering is preserved by the values of the $c^*$ function:

$$c^*(h, e) = 3/4 > c^*(h, e') = 1/2 > c^*(h, e'') = 1/4.$$

The $c^*(h, e)$ function will not, in general, have these values when defined over a language $L$ whose quantifiers range over an infinite number of individuals,

## Probability and Predictive Inference

although the $c^*$ function values will retain the desired ordering indicated above. The most astonishing result of taking $c^*$ values as the values of the $c^*$ function in languages $L$ whose quantifiers range over an infinite number of individuals is that the value of $c^*(h, e)$ for any generalization will always be 0. This result means that if the probability theory is interpreted in languages $L$ along the lines that Carnap has indicated, the whole conception of predictive inference as taking place through deductive inference from a projected hypothesis that has been assumed to this point is mistaken, since no generalization would be any more reasonable than any other on any evidence whatsoever. All generalizations are equally improbable in infinite $L$. That the $c^*$ value of any generalization on any evidence in a language whose quantifiers range over an infinite number of individuals is 0 follows from the way in which $m^*$ is defined. Consider the language $L^*$ described above. The generalization $(\forall x)(Bx)$ asserts that $Bx$ denotes every individual. In an infinite universe, the structure that corresponds to $(\forall x)(Bx)$ will contain only one element, the (infinite) conjunction of every assertion that $Bx$ denotes some individual in the domain of $L$. But there will be an infinite number of other structures, since $-Ba$ will belong to one distinct structure, $-Ba.-Bb$ to another distinct structure, and so on, each of these assertions belonging to a distinct structure which claims that $Bx$ denotes all the individuals except some number (1, 2, 3, . . .) of them. For any number of families of predicates in a language $L$ of infinite domain it is easy to see that there will be an infinite number of structures in $L$ other than the structure in which some generalization occurs. As was shown in the case of the probability

## Probability and Predictive Inference

function defined on the infinite set of all possible stopping points of the spinner's needle, if all of the elements of an infinite set are to be assigned the same probability function value consistently with the axioms of probability theory, that value must be 0. Hence the probability function value of any structure in infinite $L$ containing a generalization must be 0, and hence also the $c^*$ value for that generalization on any evidence. The fact that the probability interpretation does not allow the confirmation of laws has led many philosophers to conclude that the probability interpretation cannot solve problems of nondeductive inference which can be formulated as simple inductive problems. Carnap argues that this is not important because predictive inference can be handled by the probability interpretation, by-passing the deductive step to the prediction from a projected generalization. The claim that the next examined individual will be denoted by some property may belong (and usually belongs) to an infinite number of structures on any evidence, and hence its $c^*$ function value need not be 0. In other words, Carnap asserts that scientists do not predict (or need not predict) on the basis of generalizations, but may give a well-confirmed prediction that some individual will have a certain property on the basis that all past examined individuals have had that property.

The values of any $c(h, e)$ function in a language $L$ of infinite domain are calculated by a limit procedure on the basis of values of $c(h, e)$ in finite languages as the domains increase. This procedure is too complicated to review here, but it results in the following special formula for the $c(h, e)$ value in $L$ of infinite domain where $h$ is the prediction that the next examined

## Probability and Predictive Inference

individual will have the property represented by $Gx$ when the evidence $e$ is that all $n$ examined individuals have the property $Gx$, and no individuals are known not to have the property:

$$c(h, e) = \frac{n + \lambda/k}{n + \lambda}.$$

$k$ in this formula stands for the number of predicates in the family of predicates from which $Gx$ is taken. $\lambda$ is a parameter which defines the measure function adopted in the infinite case, and hence the values of any specific $c(h, e)$ function. $c^*(h, e)$ in $L$, for example, is that $c(h, e)$ function whose values are determined by a special choice ($\lambda^*$) for the parameter $\lambda$.

If $\lambda$ is chosen equal to 0, and $h$ and $e$ are as above, then the resulting degree of confirmation function will have the value 1. Choosing $\lambda = 0$ is in effect adopting a policy that leads immediately to predicting a property to occur again any time that its presence but not its absence is noted in evidence. But this policy is incautious. If a die is shown and tossed, and comes up a 3, this $c(h, e)$ function would lead immediately to the prediction that the next toss must also come up a 3. Such a policy obviously violates the criterion of success in certain simple cases. At the other extreme, a choice of $\lambda = \infty$ means that we should not change our minds about degree of confirmation no matter how much evidence was acquired, so that this choice would violate the criterion that nondeductive rules should be sensitive to the facts given in any application. It seems clear, therefore, that $\lambda$ should be chosen as some positive, finite number that will represent a suitable compromise between the a priorism of $\lambda = \infty$ and the rash policy provided by $\lambda = 0$.

Discussion of the exact choice of $\lambda$ to define

*Probability and Predictive Inference*

$c^*(h, e)$ in $L$ is still continuing, as well as exploration of further formulae for computing values of $c^*(h, e)$ when the evidence reports the occurrence of complex properties which may be defined from properties occurring in more than one family in $L$. An interesting suggestion by John Kemeny (in [K1]) is that the choice of $\lambda$ should not be regarded as a fixed parameter in $L$, but should be chosen for each predictive inference as a function of certain characteristics of the evidence.

There are, of course, serious difficulties in the programme of applying the calculus of probability to simple inductive and predictive problems. With respect to Carnap's programme, the solution of predictive problems is so sensitive to the choice of language $L$ and the value adopted for $\lambda$ that many philosophers have regarded the programme as having small hope of success unless choices for $L$ and $\lambda$ can be proposed which do not violate the success criterion for simple examples. The really crucial difficulty with the probability approach to inductive problems is its corrosive conclusion that all general statements are equally probable on any evidence, and that simple inductive problems cannot be solved by nondeductive rules which choose one of the hypotheses as the more reasonable. So the use of probability theory seems to result in the claim that problems of simple inductive inference involving alternative hypotheses that are generalizations are really pseudo-problems, since the goal of solving simple predictive problems can be accomplished without formulating explicitly any general hypotheses. The argument that solutions to simple inductive problems involving general hypotheses are not required for scientific method is both novel and interesting, but because it contrasts sharply

## *Probability and Predictive Inference*

with traditional views about the importance of scientific laws it suggests so many ramified arguments about the philosophy of science that its consequences will not be explored here. It should be obvious that there is a great deal of work to be done before a quantitative measure of the reasonableness of alternative generalizations on given evidence can be completely dismissed.

**Further Reading**

Probability theory over finite sets is axiomatized and developed for students of deductive logic in [S12], pp. 274–291. A more complete but unaxiomatized treatment is given in [F1]. Full mathematical treatment of probability theory as an extension of set theory is to be found in [C8] and [P1]. Carnap's application of probability theory to nondeductive inference was first given comprehensive treatment in [C1] and [C2]. Important revisions in these treatments are announced in [C3], pp. 859–1017. A good introduction to Carnap's ideas may be found in [K1], and discussions of the consequences of his approach are collected in [S8].

## Chapter Four

# STATISTICAL INFERENCE

In the past two chapters simple inductive and simple predictive problems have been discussed in which the evidence was such that it could be characterized by a conjunction of sentences reporting that some property was true of every individual examined in the evidence. Partly because of the fact that *every* individual examined had the property, the *order* in which the evidence was accumulated was thought to be irrelevant. A significant change is now made in the kind of evidence on which a nondeductive problem may be based. In the next two chapters, evidence is considered in terms of which no property can be fruitfully ascribed to every examined individual because the point of gathering evidence is to study the way in which two properties chosen in advance are associated. If there are some individuals having one property but not the other, and vice versa, then no hypothesis about the relationship between them may be available other than a statistical generalization. But the order in which evidence is gathered for a statistical generalization is relevant. If we notice that 1/2 of all $A$'s are $B$'s, then we may regard this evidence quite differently if we find an entrenched third property $C$ such that all and

## Statistical Inference

only the $A$'s which are also $B$'s have it than if we can discover no such property.

The development and use of probability functions for solving statistical nondeductive problems is associated historically with games of chance. A die, or coin, can be manufactured out of homogeneous material so as to be symmetrical in such ways that with a suitable tossing mechanism the outcome of a single toss of such a die or coin cannot be controlled. For such a coin, on the supposition that only one out of two possible outcomes is possible given the tossing mechanism ($u_1$ = heads, and $u_2$ = tails), the function $P\{u_1\} = P\{u_2\} = 1/2$ seems a reasonable mathematical abstraction of the behaviour expected of the coin. This is completely non-controversial in that all mathematicians acquainted with the manufacturing process and satisfied that it had produced a 'fair' coin would make this assignment of probability function values. We can see that such assignments are closely related to finite examples involving the spinner when the intervals in which the spinner's needle may stop are taken as equal in length.

There is, however, considerable controversy about how to *interpret* the assignment $P\{u_1\} = 1/2$. On one interpretation it is held that this probability function value abstracts the property of the coin and tossing procedure that a head on any toss is as probable as a tail (so that if one bets that a head will appear on the next toss of the coin he should bet at even odds in a fair wager), while on another interpretation this measure function abstracts the property that about 1/2 of all of the tosses of the coin (if it is tossed for a long time) will result in heads. The difference in these two interpretations is reflected in gambling behaviour. A

## *Statistical Inference*

man who has just seen twenty heads result from the first twenty tosses of such a coin should expect heads no more than tails on the next toss if he accepts the first interpretation, while on the second interpretation he should expect more tails than heads in the next few tosses and should expect a tail more than a head on the next toss. In practice, this uneasiness about what behaviour is actually described by $P\{u_1\} = 1/2$ is complicated by our tendency to suspect that something may have been wrong with the manufacturing process after all if a coin to which we have assigned $P\{u_1\} = 1/2$ keeps on turning up heads, even though this is *compatible* with a good manufacturing process and the assignment of a measure function leading to the probability function value $P\{u_1\} = 1/2$. If the philosophical problem of relating the mathematical assignment $P\{u_1\} = 1/2$ to the experienced behaviour of coins is hardly resolved, the success of gambling houses based on games whose expected earnings are calculated by applications of the probability calculus are sufficient to demonstrate that the formal theory of probability has useful applications, if only to those games where the manufacturing process behind the game is controlled by the gambler. The interesting and controversial applications of probability theory are to cases where the nature of what corresponds to the manufacturing process is not known. Is it, for example, legitimate to extend probability theory to abstractions of natural phenomena? Here the nature of the analogous manufacturing process is not known, and so the application of measure functions must be more tentative and cautious.

Suppose that a coin of the variety just considered is compared to a coin that is manufactured out of

*Statistical Inference*

inhomogeneous material in such a way that $m'\{u_1'\} = 3/4$, and $m'\{u_2'\} = 1/4$ seems a measure function leading to a reasonable probability function value for describing its expected behaviour. Call the first coin $F$ and the second coin $C$. $U_1 = \{u_1, u_2\}$, and $U_1' = \{u_1', u_2'\}$ are the two universe sets, and appropriate probability functions are then defined over them by the techniques of the last chapter. Let $F$ and $C$ be tossed and their manufacturing process be studied until there is no doubt that these measure functions are appropriate. Now suppose that one of the two coins is lost, but it is not known which because the manufacturing process was such that the coins appear the same under any simple visual test that can be devised except for tests relating to the different behaviour expected of them which is abstracted by their probability functions. It is proposed that the remaining coin be flipped a number of times to determine whether it is $F$ or $C$. How are the coins expected to behave? The possible results for two tosses of each can be represented by the sets $U_2 = \{\langle u_1, u_1\rangle, \langle u_1, u_2\rangle, \langle u_2, u_1\rangle, \langle u_2, u_2\rangle\}$ and $U_2' = \{\langle u_1', u_1'\rangle, \langle u_1', u_2'\rangle, \langle u_2', u_1'\rangle, \langle u_2', u_2'\rangle\}$. One expects that appropriate measure functions for these two sets should be related to the measure functions on $U_1$ and $U_1'$. The clue is provided by considering $P\{\langle u_1, u_2\rangle, \langle u_1, u_1\rangle\}$. This is the probability of getting a head on the first toss followed by a tail on the second toss or getting a head on the first toss followed by a head on the second toss. But this is the same as the probability of getting a head on the first toss of $F$ which we already know to be 1/2. So $P\{\langle u_1, u_2\rangle, \langle u_1, u_1\rangle\} = P\{\langle u_1, u_2\rangle\} + P\{\langle u_1, u_1\rangle\} = 1/2$. Similarly, $P\{\langle u_2, u_2\rangle, \langle u_1, u_2\rangle\} = P\{\langle u_2, u_2\rangle\} + P\{\langle u_1, u_2\rangle\} = 1/2$, as the set $\{\langle u_2, u_2\rangle, \langle u_1, u_2\rangle\}$ represents the event of getting a

## Statistical Inference

tail on the second toss. Using these identities, one can find that $m\{\langle u_1, u_1\rangle\} = m\{\langle u_1, u_2\rangle\} = m\{\langle u_2, u_1\rangle\} = m\{\langle u_2, u_2\rangle\} = 1/4$. The same kind of calculation for $U_2'$ defines a measure function $m'$, except that $P\{\langle u_1', u_2'\rangle, \langle u_1', u_1'\rangle\}$ (the probability of getting a head on the first toss) is 3/4, and so on. The following measure functions (and subsequent $P$ functions by Definition 1) are thus obtained for $U_2$ and $U_2'$: $m\{\langle u_1, u_1\rangle\} = m\{\langle u_1, u_2\rangle\} = m\{\langle u_2, u_1\rangle\} = m\{\langle u_2, u_2\rangle\} = 1/4$ for $U_2$; $m'\{\langle u_1', u_1'\rangle\} = 9/16$, $m'\{\langle u_1', u_2'\rangle\} = m\{\langle u_2', u_1'\rangle\} = 3/16$, and $m'\{\langle u_2', u_2'\rangle\} = 1/16$ for $U_2'$. Let the unknown coin be tossed twice. Since $u_1$ and $u_1'$ represent a head resulting from a toss of $F$ and a head resulting from a toss of $C$ respectively, and $u_2$ and $u_2'$ tails resulting from such tosses, the result of the two tosses will be represented by a pair from $U_2$ or a pair from $U_2'$. We do not *know* which pair represents the true situation, but try to guess which pair on the basis of the two tosses. Suppose that two heads turn up. This is either correctly represented by $\langle u_1, u_1\rangle$ or $\langle u_1', u_1'\rangle$. $\langle u_1, u_1\rangle$ has probability 1/4 of occurring if the coin is $F$, and $\langle u_1', u_1'\rangle$ has probability 9/16 of occurring if the coin is $C$. Thus two heads are more likely to be truly represented by $\langle u_1', u_1'\rangle$ than by $\langle u_1, u_1\rangle$ if it is equally likely that $F$ or $C$ has been tossed. *On the assumption that the most probable event is the one which has occurred,* we should guess that the coin is coin $C$. The assumption that we should choose that hypothesis (or any of several, if there are more than one) on the basis of which we most expect an observed event is a crude way of stating the *principle of maximum likelihood* which plays an important role in statistical inference. The reader may verify that any other result than two heads is more probable if the coin is $F$ than

## Statistical Inference

if it is $C$, so that unless the two tosses result in heads, we would guess that the coin is, in fact, coin $F$.

It was a feature of this sample statistical problem that the experimental result (the two tosses of the coin are a very simple experiment which is run to decide between the two hypotheses concerning the identity of the coin) was such that it could be considered as a member of $U_2$ or $U_2'$. We might represent the possible outcomes of the experiment as being the members of a set $U'' = \{\langle \text{head, head} \rangle, \langle \text{head, tail} \rangle, \langle \text{tail, head} \rangle, \langle \text{tail, tail} \rangle\}$. The two hypotheses may then be represented by $F$ and $C$. Then the problem of statistical inference is to choose a function which selects one of the possible hypotheses ($F$ or $C$) for each member of $U''$. The maximum likelihood function was $f$: $f\langle \text{head, head} \rangle = C$, and $f\langle \text{head, tail} \rangle = f\langle \text{tail, head} \rangle = f\langle \text{tail, tail} \rangle = F$. This was chosen because $\langle \text{head, head} \rangle$ was more likely to be $\langle u_1', u_1' \rangle$ if $C$ was the true hypothesis than it was to be $\langle u_1, u_1 \rangle$ if $F$ was the true hypothesis. A similar argument decides the other values of $f$. An important feature of experimental results in statistical inference is that they represent data which might be observed if any one of a variety of hypotheses is true.

In the coin experiment, the results $\langle \text{head, tail} \rangle$ and $\langle \text{tail, head} \rangle$ from the set $U''$ appear to be equivalent in their evidential significance. Interpreted as $\langle u_1, u_2 \rangle$ and $\langle u_2, u_1, \rangle$ they have the same probability of occurring if $F$ is true, and interpreted as $\langle u_1', u_2' \rangle$ and $\langle u_2', u_1' \rangle$, they have the same probability of occurring if $C$ is true. This suggests a way of simplifying the experiment. (Our actual example is so simple that this gain may appear ridiculous, but its extension to complex problems is often an important time-saver.) A partition of a set $U$ is any set of non-overlapping subsets of $U$ whose

## Statistical Inference

set union is $U$. Thus a set of pairwise disjoint sets $\{P_0, \ldots, P_n\}(P_i \subset U$ for all $i = 1, \ldots, n)$ is a *partition* of $U$ if and only if $\bigcup_i P_i = U$. $P_0 = \{\langle u_1, u_1 \rangle\}$, $P_1 = \{\langle u_1, u_2 \rangle, \langle u_2, u_1 \rangle\}$, $P_2 = \{\langle u_2, u_2 \rangle\}$ is consequently a partition of $U_2$, and each member of this partition represents the event of getting 0, 1, or 2 tails in the two-toss experiment. $P(P_0) = 1/4$, $P(P_1) = 1/2$, and $P(P_2) = 1/4$, since $P_0$ and $P_2$ are identical to subsets of $U_2$ whose $P$ value has already been calculated, and $P(P_1)$ may be easily calculated by application of the theory of probability to the subsets of $U_2$.

The partition $\{P_0, P_1, P_2\}$ enables a simplification of the data to be made. We may calculate a similar partition $\{P_0', P_1', P_2'\}$ of $U_2'$. Now instead of noticing the *order* of heads and tails, we merely note the *number* of tails which appear in the two tosses. This may be done as the tosses are made, or the number may be calculated from an experimental result in which the order of the heads and tails has been observed. A number which is calculated from complex observations as a means of expressing some important property of the observations for the purposes of statistical inference is known as a *statistic*. Many books on statistics are essentially concerned with discussing ways of calculating statistics in this sense for the purpose of representing the important features of a complex set of observations. In the case of the coin example, the *statistic* that represents the *number* of tails in the two tosses is called a *sufficient statistic* for guessing whether the coin is $F$ or $C$ because using it with the maximum likelihood function $f'$ ($f'(0) = C$, $f'(1) = f'(2) = F$) defined on the set of statistics giving simply the number of tails on the two tosses leads to the same choice of

## Statistical Inference

$F$ or $C$ as the correct hypothesis as the function $f$ does on a full description of the data. In more complicated statistical inferences, considerable difficulties in calculation can be avoided by reducing a full description of the data that is accumulated in experimentation to a set of statistics which is also a set of sufficient statistics, that is, a set over which a function can be defined which is equivalent to a function describing the acceptable statistical inferences made on a full description of the data.

We may define *simple statistical inference* as a special case of simple inductive inference. A simple statistical inference is a choice between two equally likely statistical hypotheses $H_1$ and $H_2$ each of which is an assignment of a probability function to a universe set. The universe sets $U$ and $U'$ to which $H_1$ and $H_2$ assign probability functions are of the same cardinality. Elements of these two sets are correlated so that paired elements are in some way observationally indistinguishable. The choice is made between $H_1$ and $H_2$ on the basis of an experiment each of whose relevant outcomes is represented by a statistic which represents some state of affairs which is more likely if $H_1$ is true than if $H_2$ is true, or vice versa. (It is possible that one or more correlated elements of $U$ and $U'$ will be equally likely given the hypotheses. If an experiment results in an event which is either of these elements, then the choice between hypotheses is not made, or it is decided by a random choice between them. These complications are overlooked here.) The experiment must be carried out under circumstances that do not favour one hypothesis over the other. A maximum likelihood function is then defined from each possible statistic of the experiment to the hypothesis whose truth would make its occurrence most

## Statistical Inference

likely. This total situation may be described by a set of seven elements $\langle H_1, U, H_2, U', E_i, K, f \rangle$. $H_1$ and $H_2$ are the hypotheses to be chosen between, $U$ and $U'$ are sets of equal cardinality over which $H_1$ and $H_2$ define probability functions, and $E_i$ is a set of $n$ statistics ($i = 1, \ldots, n$) each of which represents an experimental datum that could be gathered from experimental procedure $K$ whose possible outcomes are such that they are compatible with both hypothesis $H_1$ and hypothesis $H_2$, but each outcome of procedure $K$ is more likely to occur on the supposition that just one of $H_1$ or $H_2$ is true. Procedure $K$ is such that if $H_1$ is true its outcomes will exhibit the behaviour expected when $H_1$ is true, and if $H_2$ is true its outcomes will exhibit the behaviour expected on that hypothesis. $f$ is the maximum likelihood function from the members of $E_i$ to $H_1$ and $H_2$ which represents the appropriate statistical inference. In our example, $K$ was the way of flipping coins that had led to the assignment of $H_1$ and $H_2$ describing the expected behaviour of the coins under repeated tossing. Simple statistical inference satisfying this definition is non-controversial, in that the maximum likelihood function satisfies all of the properties desired of rules for inductive inference, and it is compatible with the intuition of virtually every philosopher and statistician.

Controversy about statistical inference is largely a result of attempting a method of defining appropriate functions correlating statistics derived from experimental results with statistical hypotheses when one or more of the rather stringent assumptions of simple statistical inference are relaxed.

The probability that some $E_i$ will be the experimental result when the hypothesis $H_1$ is true is known

*Statistical Inference*

as the *likelihood* of $E_i$ on hypothesis $H_1$. In the coin example with $H_1 = F$ and $H_2 = C$, $E_i$ had three members, 0, 1, or 2 corresponding to the appearance of 0, 1, or 2 tails in the result of experimental procedure $K$. Now intuitively one would feel more certain that $C$ was the true hypothesis if 0 tails were observed than that $F$ was the true hypothesis if 1 tail were observed. This is reflected in the fact that the difference between the likelihood of 0 tails on hypothesis $C$ (9/16) and the likelihood of 0 tails on hypothesis $F$ (4/16) is much greater than the difference between the likelihood of 1 tail on hypothesis $F$ (8/16) and the likelihood of 1 tail on hypothesis $C$ (6/16). We might thus let the likelihood ratio between the hypothesis adopted and the hypothesis rejected represent our relative confidence in choosing $H_1$ or $H_2$ on a given statistic. Now let the statistical inference in the example be replaced by a statistical inference with the same hypotheses, but one in which the procedure $K$ is replaced by a procedure $K'$ which differs from $K$ in that the test coin is tossed three times instead of twice. Now $E_i'$ is {0, 1, 2, 3}, the element chosen to represent the experimental result depending on whether 0, 1, 2, or 3 tails appear in three tosses. The likelihoods of getting 0, 1, 2, or 3 tails in three tosses of coin $F$ are 8/64, 24/64, 24/64, and 8/64, respectively, while the likelihoods of getting 0, 1, 2, or 3 tails in three tosses of coin $C$ are 27/64, 27/64, 9/64, and 1/64, respectively. The maximum likelihood function is consequently $f$: $f(0) = f(1) = C$, and $f(2) = f(3) = F$. All of the likelihood ratios are greater than the smallest likelihood ratio for any outcome of two tosses, which means that any inference based on three tosses is one we can feel more certain about than the most certain inference

## Statistical Inference

based on two tosses. Indeed, the increases in the likelihood ratios are taken by many statisticians as a good measure of *how much* the experiment with three tosses increases the probability that the accepted hypothesis is the correct one. (See [G2], p. 63.) We choose $C$ or $F$ when we have all tails or no tail in either experiment, but the likelihood ratios for the choices on three tosses are higher. Summarizing, if we toss the coin three times and choose between $H_1$ and $H_2$ by means of the maximum likelihood function, we are more certain of choosing between $H_1$ and $H_2$ correctly than if we choose between $H_1$ and $H_2$ by means of the maximum likelihood function on the basis of only two tosses. In general, the more data one accumulates, the more reliable his statistics are (in the sense of showing more behaviour of evidence), the higher the likelihood ratio for the choice becomes, and the more certain one can be of having chosen correctly among the alternatives.

The likelihood ratio test which has been described here can be extended to a sequential test. It might be decided, for example, that the likelihood ratio of the accepted hypothesis should be at least 9 to 1, or some other fairly high ratio. (Intuitively, this would correspond to about 90% confidence that the correct choice had been made. The ratio adopted as a criterion seems to depend on a subjective choice related to the intuitive *seriousness* of the consequences of making a wrong choice. This has some interesting consequences for scientific method that are discussed in [R5].) Suppose, in the coin example, that the likelihood ratio on some given experimental result is always given with the likelihood of $H_1$ (the coin is $F$) as the numerator, and the likelihood of $H_2$ (the coin is $C$) as the denominator. Then if the likelihood ratio is 9/1 or

## Statistical Inference

greater, $H_1$ is adopted, and if the likelihood ratio is 1/9 or less, $H_2$ is adopted. If the likelihood ratio is between 1/9 and 9/1, neither hypothesis is adopted, but more experiments are run in an effort to obtain a likelihood ratio that will permit a choice to be made. This is the idea behind a *sequential test*. A *sequential test* is conducted by repeating results in some experimental set-up, stopping the experiment and making a choice only when the likelihood ratio falls below or exceeds certain fixed ratios. In the case of two probability functions defined on finite sets whose related measure functions give different values to correlated members of the two sets, it is fairly straightforward to calculate the expected number of observations that will have to be made before a choice between $H_1$ and $H_2$ can be made by a sequential test. In the more general case of probability functions defined on infinite sets, the measure functions may be so close in value (although still distinct) that there is no expected number of observations that will permit a definite choice to be made between the hypotheses.

No amount of data can ever enable one to be sure that he has chosen correctly (except in some trivial finite cases) between rival statistical hypotheses. In this way, the test of a statistical hypothesis is quite like the test of any other scientific hypothesis. One cannot accumulate enough data to deduce a general hypothesis from the data. On the other hand, two different non-statistical hypotheses may decisively confront a given experiment whose results must be a counter-example to one of them. Two statistical hypotheses can normally confront a given experiment in only a weaker sense, the situation being that an experiment can at most show either that the statistics of the

## Statistical Inference

experiment are extremely unlikely to be repeated in a similar experiment, or that one of the hypotheses is in fact not a correct abstraction of expected behaviour of some kind. Many epistemologists have been tempted to suppose that the decisiveness of some results used to choose between non-statistical hypotheses is really spurious, since we may never be certain that any observation has been made correctly. These epistemologists have consequently suggested that *all* non-deductive scientific inference is really statistical inference, the case considered in previous chapters as non-statistical being merely the limit case where the conclusion of statistical inference is that one hypothesis is not a correct abstraction of expected behaviour because the probability of the facts being repeated is arbitrarily close to 1.

Now we can review the relationship between $H_1$, $H_2$, $E_i$, and $K$ in a simple statistical inference. If $H_1$, $H_2$, $E_i$, and $K$ are *given* in a simple statistical problem, the maximum likelihood function decides between $H_1$ and $H_2$ as before. If, on the other hand, $H_1$ and $H_2$ are given, but we may choose $E_i$ and $K$ so as to be quite certain that we have chosen correctly, then $E_i$ and $K$ can be selected through the use of statistical considerations to obtain the desired result. The situation where $E_i$ and $K$ are *given* may arise in practical situations because $E_i$ and $K$ may represent old data upon which some decision is to be made. For the purposes of illustrating experimental problems, suppose each toss of the coin in the example discussed costs ten-pence, and suppose that the problem is to make the best choice between $H_1$ and $H_2$ that can be made without spending more than three pounds. Then some sequential test may be called for. Of course, sequential

## Statistical Inference

tests are not possible where the experimental set-up is such that enough results may not be obtained from it. The appropriate ways of choosing $E_i$ and $K$ under various constraints and for various choices of alternative hypotheses $H_1$ and $H_2$ are discussed in various textbooks on statistical inference. The important point here is that the assumption that $f$ indicates the *correct choice* between $H_1$ and $H_2$ given $E_i$ and $K$ is potentially misleading. $f$ may only indicate which choice is most reasonable, and if they are equally reasonable may provide grounds for withholding a choice until a decisive experiment can be performed. The appropriateness of a maximum likelihood function for solving simple statistical problems involving probability distributions defined on finite sets only is widely accepted and difficult to question.

It was demonstrated earlier that a measure function defined on the elements of a universe set $U$ which proves satisfactory for defining a probability function on a finite set will not by itself prove satisfactory for defining a probability function on an infinite set. An analogous problem arises for statistical inference when the requirement on simple statistical inference that the two sets $U$ and $U$ be finite is relaxed. Suppose we are interested in choosing between two probability functions $H_1$ and $H_2$ defined over infinite sets $U$ and $U'$. Let $E_i$ be a specific outcome of $K$ which might be either an element $u_i$ of $U$ or an element $u_i'$ of $U'$. To use the maximum likelihood function, we must calculate the likelihood of $u_i$ if $H_1$ is true, and the likelihood of $u_i'$ if $H_2$ is true. As we have seen in the case of the probability function defined for the universe set of all points on which the needle of the spinnner may stop, the probability function value of all of the

## Statistical Inference

*elements* of an infinite set may well be (and often is) 0. If $H_1$ assigns the value 0 to $u$ of $U$, and $H_2$ assigns the value 0 to $u'$ of $U'$, then both the likelihood of $u$ given $H_1$ and of $u'$ given $H_2$ are 0, and the maximum likelihood function cannot enable us to choose between $H_1$ and $H_2$, although one of these hypotheses may be much more reasonable than the other.

To discuss briefly the way in which choices between hypotheses defined on infinite sets can be made, we return to the case of the spinner. Suppose that in attempting to construct the spinner we make an experimental model which has a defective bearing such that it causes the spinner to have the following properties: the needle may still stop at any point of the dial, but because of the bearing defect it will tend to stop in one area of the dial. It can be further supposed that the bearing defect is such that the increased friction of the needle against the bearing varies continuously and symmetrically about some point, i.e. there is a point on the dial when the friction is greatest, and the friction diminishes continuously and symmetrically on either side of this point. A probability function could be given to abstract the probability that the needle will stop at any point. Since the needle may still stop at any point of the dial, we take the universe set to be the set of all points on the circumference of the dial, and so $P(U) = 1$ as in the case of the spinner without defect. To further characterize the probability function, we need to know the point $\mu$ at which the friction is greatest. The probability function can then be defined (because of the symmetry of the increased friction around $\mu$) for intervals which have $\mu$ as their centre point, the various probability function values indicating how probable it is that the needle will come

## *Statistical Inference*

to rest on a point which is an element of such an interval. The interval centred on $\mu$ which is thus assigned a probability function value of 1/2 will be less than half the circumference of the defective spinner's dial due to the significance of the increased friction which is greatest at $\mu$. How much less than 1/2 of the circumference of the defective spinner's dial it will be is dependent on the increase of friction around $\mu$. The greater the increase, the shorter the interval that will be assigned the value 1/2. The less the increase, the longer the interval, until it coincides with half the circumference in the limiting case of the bearing without defect, that is, in the case of the spinner proper. Consequently, the severity of the additional friction caused by the defect in the bearing may be designated by a single paramater $\sigma$, which is a measure of the relative severity of the friction at $\mu$ caused by the defect in the bearing compared to the friction at $\mu$ in the spinner without defect.

A measure function for the defective spinner will now be developed in a fashion worth comparing with the measure function defined for the spinner proper. As in that case, the simple subsets for $U$ will be the set of all intervals and degenerate intervals which are subsets of $U$. By a similar argument to that used in the other case, we let the measure function value of any degenerate interval be 0. Then we begin by considering those nondegenerate intervals which may be said to centre on $\mu$. Any such interval can be represented as an interval $[\mu - a, \mu + a]$. The measure function values of such intervals cannot be simply the ratio of their length to the length of the circumference, since the significance of $\mu$ is that the needle has a probability greater than 1/2 of stopping in the interval $[\mu - 90°,$

## Statistical Inference

$\mu + 90°$], which has a length 1/2. How much greater the probability is depends on the value of $\sigma$, which represents how widely the increased friction is 'spread out' around $\mu$. The measure function value of the interval $[\mu - a, \mu + a]$ is thus a function dependent on $\mu$, $\sigma$, and $a$. Let $g(x, \mu, \sigma)$ be a function giving the appropriate measure function value of the arbitrary interval $[\mu - x, \mu + x]$ for the defective spinner when $\mu$ and $\sigma$ are known. This function can be given in an explicit mathematical form, but it is not given here as its explicit form is mathematically somewhat complicated. Then the measure function value of the interval $[\mu - a, \mu + a]$ is the value of the function $g(x, \mu, \sigma)$ when $a$ is substituted for $x$, that is, $g(a, \mu, \sigma)$. The measure function value of any interval which is not centred around $\mu$ may be calculated from the measure function values of the intervals which are centred around $\mu$. To show this, we may note that if $b, c$ is an interval, then its length is equal to the sum $[b, m] + [m, c]$ of the lengths of the intervals $[b, m]$ and $[m, c]$, where $m$ is between $b$ and $c$. Let $[b, c]$ be an interval not containing $\mu$ as a point which lies between $\mu$ and $\mu - 180°$. Let $\mu - r = b$, and $\mu - s = c$. Then $[\mu - r, \mu + r]$ will contain $[b, c]$, and $[b, c]$ will lie outside of $[\mu - s, \mu + s]$. Now since $\mu - r < \mu - s$, and $\mu + s < \mu + r$, we can define the intervals $[\mu - r, \mu - s]$, $[\mu + s, \mu + r]$ which are equal in length. Now $[\mu - r, \mu + r] = [\mu - s, \mu + s] + [\mu - r, \mu - s] + [\mu + s, \mu + r] = [\mu - s, \mu + s] + 2[\mu - r, \mu - s] = [\mu - s, \mu + s] + 2[b, c]$. Solving this for $[b, c]$, we obtain $[b, c] = [\mu - r, \mu + r] - [\mu - s, \mu + s]/2$. We now find the measure function value of $[b, c]$ by substituting the measure function values of the centred intervals into the right-hand side of this equation.

## Statistical Inference

Similarly, to find the measure function value of any interval between $\mu - 180°$ and $\mu$, or between $\mu$ and $\mu + 180°$, we find it as the solution of an algebraic equation in terms of the lengths of centred intervals, using the property of symmetry around $\mu$, and then substituting the values of $g(x, \mu, \sigma)$ for the centred intervals in the equation in order to get the measure function value of the original interval. An interval containing $\mu$ which is not centred on $\mu$ can be evaluated as the sum of an interval centred on $\mu$ and an interval not containing $\mu$. An interval containing the point $\mu - 180°$ can be determined as the sum of the two intervals $[a, \mu + 180°]$ and $[\mu - 180°, b]$. Thus by means of the intervals centred on $\mu$ and the function $g(x, \mu, \sigma)$ we can determine a measure function value for every interval which is a subset of $U$. Now a probability function can be defined on $U$ by Definition 1.

Having defined such a probability function for a defective spinner, the difficulties of statistical inference for infinite probability distribution can be considered. Suppose that we have a defective spinner, and a probability function derived from the function $g(x, \mu, \sigma)$ which we are satisfied is an accurate abstraction of the expected behaviour of the spinner's needle when spun sufficiently hard with the fingers. Suppose further that the mark used to distinguish the point $\mu$ on the dial is suddenly smudged or erased, although the defective spinner can be otherwise identified, and we may even recall roughly where $\mu$ is. Let two hypotheses about the value of $\mu$ be adopted, $\mu = \mu'$ and $\mu = \mu''$, and let $g(x, \mu', \sigma)$ and $g(x, \mu'', \sigma)$ be the functions that will define the resulting alternative probability distributions $H_1$ and $H_2$ for the problem of statistical inference. $K$ is to be the experiment of three

## Statistical Inference

spins of the needle and $E_i$ ($i = 1, 2, \ldots$) to be the possible combinations of three stopping-places of the needle on three spins. Let $K$ be performed and some $E_i$ noted. How can a choice between $H_1$ and $H_2$ be made? To follow the procedure used for tossing coins earlier, we should determine a probability distribution over the $E_i$ for $H_1$ and $H_2$. But as the likelihood of the needle stopping exactly on any point is 0, the likelihood of the needle stopping on exactly any three points is also 0. This is true for both $H_1$ and $H_2$. Therefore, the likelihood of the exact result will not solve the problem of statistical inference. The problem of comparing finite evidence to probability distributions of infinite sets is thus very complex. In fact, there is no general solution to this problem comparable to that of the maximum likelihood function for probability distributions defined on finite universe sets. Proceeding in a particular case of statistical inference involving infinite universe sets, a statistician will try to find a function from the evidence to the probability distributions that may be called an *estimator*. An estimator compares a *statistic* calculated from the evidence with a parameter of the theoretical probability distributions. (In more complicated cases, estimators may have to compare several statistics to several parameters.) Many desirable characteristics for estimators may be cited, although the precise characteristics to adopt in defining *estimators* is a matter of some dispute among statisticians. One characteristic generally agreed upon is that the statistic calculated from the evidence should gradually coincide with the (true) parameter of the theoretical probability distribution as the evidence size tends to infinity. To return to our example, the only difference in the hypotheses is

## Statistical Inference

the value assigned to $\mu$. The significance of $\mu$ provides the clue to a reasonable estimator from the $E_t$ to $H_1$ and $H_2$. Since $\mu$ is the point where the friction is greatest, we would expect the needle's exact stopping-points to cluster around $\mu$ if the defective spinner is spun over and over. Thus the estimator function determines the arithmetic mean stopping-place of the specific points on which the needle stops (this will be well defined for three spins unless the needle stops at three points equidistant from each other around the dial) and compares this with the value of the parameter $\mu$ in the theoretical distribution. For simplicity's sake, let $H_1$ have $\mu = 180°$, and $H_2$ have $\mu = 240°$. Let the spinner stop at the points 100°, 250°, and 160° in its three spins. The mean stopping-point is 100 + 250 + 160/3 = 170. Since 170° is closer to 180° than 240°, the estimator function would choose $H_1$ as the correct hypothesis on the basis of this evidence. Unlike the finite case discussed earlier, the estimator function may not always permit a choice between $H_1$ and $H_2$. If the needle stopped on the points 175°, 243°, and 212°, then the mean stopping-place would be 210°, the point midway between the parameters of the alternative hypotheses. As in the finite case, it may be necessary to make a decision (reflecting our confidence in the choice) as to how much closer to the value of one parameter than the other a calculated statistic should be before a choice between $H_1$ and $H_2$ is made. The example of the defective spinner and unknown $\mu$ may be used to generalize *simple statistical inference* to the infinite case. If the choice in statistical inference is between two distinct probability distributions which differ only in the value of a single parameter, and a suitable estimator is available, then the statistical

## Statistical Inference

inference between the hypotheses on the basis of given evidence may well be considered sound. We can therefore consider this case a more complex case of simple statistical inference.

Suppose that the requirements of simple statistical inference are relaxed still further. If the alternative hypotheses are specific probability distributions, but they are more than two in number, the case can be solved for a finite number in the last resort by solving all of the simple statistical inferences which result from taking them two at a time, and then comparing results. There are, of course, much simpler procedures for most specific cases. But statistical inference becomes generally unsolvable when the number of alternative hypotheses becomes infinite. The most tractable case is where the alternative hypotheses differ only in the value of a single parameter. In the case of the defective spinner whose $\mu$ is unknown, no alternative *specific* hypotheses may be specified because none seem particularly reasonable, but we may wish to guess at the value of $\mu$. The same estimator may be used, but a considerable number of spins may be required before we feel that the guess is close to the true theoretical parameter. In simple statistical inference, however, a very small number of spins may enable us to make a confident choice between alternative hypotheses. Now suppose that we have a spinner whose $\mu$ and $\sigma$ are both unknown. The problem is considerably more difficult. Almost any number of spins would be equally compatible with some alternative hypotheses choosing quite different values of $\mu$ and $\sigma$. And, of course, if we allow that the spinner's defects might be more complex, that is, that bearing defects may occur in more than one place, the problem

## Statistical Inference

of determining a probability distribution on the basis of a small number of spins becomes indeterminate. It is equivalent to trying to solve algebraic equations in which there are too many unknowns to permit a definite solution. Books on statistical inference often contain as their only emotional passages pleas against research which simply accumulates data and then is submitted to a statistician who is supposed to find the true hypothesis that accounts for it. As should now be clear, intelligent experimental design usually involves finding an experimental design $K$ that will economically discriminate between plausible given hypotheses.

It is interesting to notice in connection with the discussion of statistical inference that a problem often set by philosophers to be solved by nondeductive rules is in fact one of the most difficult problems of statistical inference. If one notices that $m/n$ of all observed $A$'s are $B$'s, one may wonder about the ratio of all $A$'s to all $B$'s. This is usually equivalent to asking which one of an infinite number of statistical hypotheses is the correct description of the conditional probability of being a $B$ when something is an $A$, and in this form it involves a choice between an infinite number of alternative statistical hypotheses, and may consequently not have a reasonable solution. The usual solution suggested is to make an estimate of the true ratio close to the observed ratio $m/n$, but all of the suggested particular methods of doing this in the general case have encountered undesirable consequences in certain intuitive examples.

Nondeductive rules can perhaps only *solve* problems of deciding which among explicitly formulated hypotheses is most reasonable on given evidence, not those of picking from all the hypotheses which *might*

## Statistical Inference

be formulated consistently with the given evidence the most reasonable hypothesis accounting for the evidence. The set of all possible hypotheses is in many cases not even well defined.

Goodman's entrenchment proposals have a natural extension to the problem of statistical inference. In a sense all proposed possible values of various parameters in a functional form may be equally well entrenched, so that no choice among conflicting statistical hypotheses differing only in the values of their measure functions can be made in terms of the entrenchment rules. It is in this situation that statistical rules are used to define correct statistical inference. But entrenchment rules may cause us to favour those *kinds* of probability distribution which have been used most often in successful statistical inference in the past. There are, in fact, a relatively small number of entrenched probability distributions (such as the normal distribution) that statisticians usually select from in attempting to fit statistical hypotheses to evidence, even though *ad hoc* distributions could be constructed to fit evidence exactly. Thus the entrenchment notion suggests that we try to fit kinds of probability distributions that have been most used in the past to otherwise recalcitrant data, choosing specific values for the parameters of such a distribution with a provisional attitude, in that an increase in the evidence will suggest (perhaps) changes in the values of these parameters without necessarily causing rejection of the kind of probability distribution that has been fitted to the evidence.

## Further Reading

There is, of course, a vast literature on statistical inference. [H3] and [N2] are lucid introductory texts. [F3], [L2], [Q1], [S11], [W1], and [W2] discuss special cases of statistical inference and some of the principles used in solving complex problems of statistical inference. [W2] is the classic work on estimators, called statistical decision functions in much of the literature after [W2], but it is mathematically advanced. The function $g(x, \mu, \sigma)$ discussed in the chapter is the important normal distribution function, discussed in most of the above, and derived by taking a symmetrical probability function in the finite case to its mathematical limit in [C8].

## Chapter Five

# BAYESIAN STATISTICAL INFERENCE

Simple statistical inference, as discussed in the last chapter, contained the seeds of a terminological confusion that has muddled discussions of the foundations of statistical inference. Hypotheses $H_1$ and $H_2$ assigned probability measures to sets $U$ and $U'$ compatibly with the axioms of probability theory, but hypotheses $H_1$ and $H_2$ were also required to be equally *likely*, and the experimental procedure $K$ was defined as one which produced a sample compatible with $H_1$ and $H_2$ such that the procedure would be more likely to provide statistics favouring $H_1$ if $H_1$ was true, and favouring $H_2$ if $H_2$ was true. This last requirement is equivalent to the requirement that the results of $K$ be in some sense *random*, that is, produced by an experimental procedure whose design favours neither $H_1$ nor $H_2$. In terms of our example, a non-random experimental design would be one which flipped the coin twice, but ignored the first tail which appeared (if any) and flipped again, since this procedure accumulates evidence in a manner that favours $C$ over $F$. A random design could be constructed using the flipping apparatus previously used to test the behaviour of coins $F$

## Bayesian Statistical Inference

and $C$. This was, in fact, used in the example to flip the coins just twice.

The coin example of simple statistical inference indicates that there are at least *three* probability notions which enter explicitly or implicitly into simple statistical inference. The probability measures that $H_1$ and $H_2$ assign to sets $U$ and $U'$ in the example are relatively easy to understand as plausible mathematical abstractions of certain kinds of observed behaviour. But the notion that the hypotheses are equally likely is a probability notion that is quite unlike the probability of a coin turning heads, since a test can easily be constructed for the latter, but no obvious test of the equal likelihood of two hypotheses is available. *Further*, the notion that the experimental procedure should produce random results as between the competing hypotheses depends on a notion that various results of the procedure should be equally probable. This notion may at least *prima facie* involve a different notion of probability than that underlying the assignment of a probability measure over a universe set.

The difficulties with justifying the assignment of equal probabilities to two hypotheses are considerable. A probability assignment over a universe set $U$ must be such that $P(U) = 1$. This is normally thought to indicate that one, and only one, subset of $U$ can be a possible interpretation of any experimental outcome of an experimental procedure designed to compare the probability distribution over $U$ with some other probability distribution. Taking {heads, tails} as the universe set for outcomes of flipping a coin may normally seem a reasonable abstraction because the possibilities of a coin landing on its side or being lost can be for practical purposes completely removed by a carefully constructed experiment. It is not at all clear what kind of a set $U$ can function as the universe set of the possible hypotheses one of which must explain some experimental outcome. In the coin example, this difficulty was minimized as far as possible. Two coins were involved whose expected behaviour was assumed previously tested and known. It was then assumed that the lost coin was equally likely to be $F$ or $C$, such an assumption being plausible in this particular case. The coins might have been marked to distinguish them from other coins but not from each other. Also, during the course of some test at a time in which the coins were not distinguished by position, or whatever, one might have been partially destroyed by dropping it in powerful acid. Under these circumstances, it might seem reasonable to suppose that one of the two hypotheses $H$ or $F$ is true, and that in some sense it is equally likely to be either before an experiment is run.

There is a serious objection to any such procedure which has been brought by statisticians who will be called *objectivistic*. Objectivists treat the theory of probability as an extension of set theory and measure theory which may be developed as an axiomatic formal system. But they argue that probability theory can only be fruitfully or meaningfully applied when its symbols abstract various properties of the physical universe, and not of our descriptions of, or hypotheses about, the physical universe.

The most important argument *for* such a position is historical: a consideration of conditions under which mathematical abstractions have proved useful in the past. According to this argument, the importance of hypotheses lies in their ability to help us describe (predict, explain, etc.) events in the physical world. If

## Bayesian Statistical Inference

we use probability theory to abstract the expected behaviour of coins in certain kinds of tossing situations, we are staying pretty close to the classical way in which mathematical hypotheses have been used to abstract the pattern of events in the physical world. To say that the probability of a certain coin turning heads under such conditions is some real number $n$ is to say something about how the coin is expected to behave in a sufficiently large number of tosses. Now there are difficulties with specifying *exactly* the *expected* behaviour, and there are notorious difficulties with the notion of 'a sufficiently large number' of tosses. The objectivist sees these difficulties as analogous to the difficulties in giving a satisfactory interpretation of any *dispositional* term in a science. The expected behaviour of the coin, so to speak, is a disposition that it has to behave in a certain way in certain situations, and although its exact behaviour in those situations is not predictable, neither is the exact behaviour of an iron filing in a magnetic field, nor the exact behaviour of an atomic particle in certain kinds of fields. If a coin is destroyed before it has been tossed a great many times, its probability of turning heads when tossed in a certain way does not disappear, since that could be defined by a subjunctive conditional like 'If this coin were to be tossed long enough, the ratio of heads to tails resulting from the tosses would come arbitrarily close to $P$(heads)', and these kinds of subjunctive conditionals are known to appear elsewhere in scientific theory. According to objectivists, probabilities should be assigned only to events which are expected to appear with a certain frequency, or a frequency arbitrarily close to it (if the probability assigned were an irrational number, then it could never

## Bayesian Statistical Inference

be reached exactly on any experimental evidence) if certain background conditions are repeated indefinitely often.

A hypothesis is either a belief or a statement, but neither of these can be fruitfully construed as an event which is repeated with a certain frequency in a great many trials. To construe a hypothesis in this way would amount to saying that $P(H_1) = 1/2$ means that if enough hypotheses like $H_1$ were to be adopted on the basis of evidence like that on which $H_1$ is adopted, then these hypotheses would be true arbitrarily closely to 1/2 of the time. The major difficulty with this account is that if it is to be put to the test, one must start counting the true and false hypotheses adopted on the basis of evidence like that on which $H_1$ is adopted, yet there are no objective grounds for deciding when statistical hypotheses are true in the general case. And, of course, pragmatic construals of hypotheses as claims are not in principle considered as true or false statements would simply rule out any such test. The objectivist position is that only the notion of events which may be observed in repeated trials of some sort can be the basis of a fruitful abstraction to the formulae of probability theory.

Objectivists consider that the only objective basis for statistical inference is a characterization of the data available from experiment, often in terms of sufficient statistics. They suppose that the possible hypotheses that are given in a statistical problem must be supplied by the 'statistical experience' of the statistician who is making the inference. To take the position that two hypotheses are equally likely or that the experimental procedure will produce random results may be appropriate given one's statistical experience, but it amounts

## Bayesian Statistical Inference

to claiming that one can think of no reason why this is not so, and considerable reason (in the best cases) why it might be so. But to assign a probability measure to a set of possible hypotheses simply because no alternative assignment can be justified is to make an assignment based on *ignorance* of the true state of affairs rather than on empirical information. The coin example is formulated by the objectivist as satisfactory because the two coins $F$ and $C$ were sufficiently tested to assure the statistician that $H_1$ and $H_2$ are reasonable abstractions of their expected behaviour. Thus he can adopt $H_1$ and $H_2$ as appropriate hypotheses for calculating the likelihoods of the various experimental results. The only features of the experiment that are formalized in formal probability theory are the probability distributions $H_1$ and $H_2$ over $U_2$ and $U_2'$, and the likelihoods of the various $E_i$ treated as identical with elements of either $U_2$ or $U_2'$. No *probabilities* for $H_1$ and $H_2$ are abstracted into the formal theory. A simple statistical inference is made without expressing the assumption that $H_1$ and $H_2$ are equally likely as probability function values in the technical sense. On this view, nondeductive *inference* is always either an intuitive mental judgment or a decision to act as though some hypothesis were true, and in neither case is the step captured in a formal calculus. This is illustrated in the following quotation from R. A. Fisher's *Statistical Methods for Research Workers* ([F3], pp. 86–88):

> For $n = 9$, the value of $x^2$ shows that $P$ is less than 0·01 and therefore the departures from proportionality are not fortuitous . . .

The *therefore* expressing inductive inference is an ex-

## Bayesian Statistical Inference

pression of the intuitive judgment that if $P$ is less than 0·01, then the chance of the departures from proportionality being fortuitous are negligible enough to be dismissed. The choice of 0·01 may be changed in another example, but the objectivist holds that its choice cannot be based on abstracted formal properties of the experimental problem, but must be based on an intuitive assessment of its pragmatic characteristics. (See discussion of the quoted passage in [N4].)

To many philosophers and statisticians, the supposition that probability theory can only be a useful device for abstracting the features of a certain kind of experimental data has the flavour of an *ad hoc* limitation, since they see no essential reason why the 'statistical experience' of the statistician should not be capable of scientific study, and consequently, subject to some useful formal abstraction. There is an important theorem of formal probability theory that lies behind attempts to extend probability theory to formalize, not only repeatable events like coin tosses but the probability of various scientific statements other than those about certain kinds of objects. This theorem is usually called *Bayes' Theorem*. (*Bayes' Theorem* is to be sharply distinguished from *Bayes' Postulate*, the unprovable assumption that all of the hypotheses being considered in a given statistical inference are equally likely.)

We can first derive *Bayes' Theorem* from formal probability theory. Let a finite collection of sets $H_i$ ($i = 1, 2, \ldots, n$) be a partition of the universe set $U$. Further, let $E$ be any subset of $U$. Let $P$ be a probability function defined on all of the subsets of $U$. *Bayes' Theorem* then gives the conditional probability

## Bayesian Statistical Inference

of any $H_i$ on $E$. To begin with, by the definition of conditional probability:

(A) $P(H_i \mid E) = \dfrac{P(H_i \frown E)}{P(E)}$ (for any $i = 1, 2, \ldots, n$).

By the same definition:

(B) $P(E \mid H_i) = \dfrac{P(E \frown H_i)}{P(H_i)}$ (for any $i = 1, 2, \ldots, n$).

Now since $(E \frown H_i) = (H_i \frown E)$ by set theory, we can substitute into (A) using the identity (B) after multiplying both sides of the latter by $P(H_i)$ to get:

(C) $P(H_i \mid E) = \dfrac{P(H_i)P(E \mid H_i)}{P(E)}$ (for any $i = 1, 2, \ldots, n$).

From set theory, $E = \bigcup_i (E \frown H_i)$, since each element of $E$ must belong also to one, and only one, member of the collection $H_i$. Therefore,

$$P(E) = P(\bigcup_i (E \frown H_i)).$$

Using the fact that the $H_i$ are pairwise disjoint along with repeated applications of axiom (2) of probability theory, we obtain:

$$P(E) = \sum_i P(E \frown H_i).$$

$P(E \frown H_i) = P(H_i)P(E \mid H_i)$ from (B), so by substitution we obtain

$P(E) = \sum_i P(H_i)P(E \mid H_i).$ Using this identity, we substitute in

## Bayesian Statistical Inference

(C) to get *Bayes' Theorem*:

$$P(H_i \mid E) = \frac{P(H_i)P(E \mid H_i)}{\sum_i P(H_i)P(E \mid H_i)} \text{ (for any } i = 1, 2, \ldots, n\text{).}$$

The significance of *Bayes' Theorem* is that if it is possible to construe the $H_i$ as the alternative hypotheses involved in some experiment, and if $E$ can be construed as the evidence, then $P(H_i \mid E)$ gives the probability that $H_i$ is true if $E$ is true. Examination of the theorem shows that this probability (sometimes called the *posterior probability* of the hypothesis $H_i$ on evidence $E$) is directly proportional to the *prior probability* $P(H_i)$ of the hypothesis. This is as we should expect. Other things being equal, if one hypothesis can be said to be most probably true before the experiment, for example, we expect it to remain most probably true after the experiment if the evidence is compatible with it. The theorem also gives the posterior probability as directly proportional to the likelihood of $E$ on $H_i$, reflecting the assumption that leads to acceptance of the maximum likelihood principle in simple statistical inference.

It is fairly easy to show that the various probabilities required for a statement of *Bayes' Theorem* can be abstracted by a probability function defined over a universe set that is consistent with the axioms of formal probability theory. This will be demonstrated here for the sample statistical inference involving hypotheses $H_1$ and $H_2$ and two throws of the coin already discussed in detail: a generalization of this procedure to other examples of simple statistical inference is straightforward. In the experiment involving the coin, two universe sets $U_2$ and $U_2'$ had probability functions

## Bayesian Statistical Inference

defined over them by the measure functions $m\{\langle u_1, u_1\rangle\} = m\{\langle u_1, u_2\rangle\} = m\{\langle u_2, u_1\rangle\} = m\{\langle u_2, u_2\rangle\} = 1/4$ and $m'\{\langle u_1', u_1'\rangle\} = 9/16$, $m'\{\langle u_1', u_2'\rangle\} = m'\{\langle u_2', u_1'\rangle\} = 3/16$, $m'\{\langle u_2', u_2'\rangle\} = 1/16$. Let the four elements of $U_2$ and the four elements of $U_2'$ be the eight elements of a new universe set $U^*$. The elements of $U^*$ thus represent the eight possible specific outcomes of two tosses of the coin whose identity is unknown. The hypothesis $H_1$ (the coin is $C$) and the hypothesis $H_2$ (the coin is $F$) are represented in the set $U^*$ by the two subsets of $U^*$ which are identical to the sets $U_2$ and $U_2'$, i.e. $H_1 = U_2'$ and $H_2 = U_2$. $\{H_1, H_2\}$ or $\{U_2', U_2\}$ is thus a partition of $U^*$. Suppose that the appropriate probability function values for $H_1$ and $H_2$ are $P(H_1)=a$, and $P(H_2) = b$, where $a + b = 1$ since $U^* = H_1 \cup H_2$. We now calculate a measure function $m^*$ for $P$ defined on $U^*$ as follows: If $\langle u_i, u_j\rangle$ ($i, j = 1, 2$) is an element of $U^*$ and $H_2$, then $m^*\{\langle u_i, u_j\rangle\} = bm\{\langle u_i, u_j\rangle\}$, and if $\langle u_i', u_j'\rangle$ is an element of $U^*$ and $H_1$, then $m^*\{\langle u_i', u_j'\rangle\} = am\{\langle u_i', u_j'\rangle\}$. Taking the sets whose only elements are single elements of $U^*$ as the simple subsets of $U^*$, we may use $m^*$ and Definition 1 to define a probability function that satisfies the axioms of the formal theory. The intuitive idea is simple. Two universe sets with appropriate measure functions are merged into a larger universe set, an adjustment in the measure function values for the original sets being made by reducing them in a ratio equivalent to their probabilities in the larger set.

We show that axiom (3) is satisfied by this technique. By the fact that $\{H_1, H_2\}$ is a partition of $U^*$ we have $P(U^*) = P(H_1) + P(H_2)$. We first evaluate $P(H_2)$. $P(H_2)$, by Definition 1, is identical to the sum of the $m^*$ values of the elements of $H_2$. Therefore,

*Bayesian Statistical Inference*

$P(H_2) = \sum_{ij} m^*\{\langle u_i, u_j \rangle\} = \sum_{ij} bm\{\langle u_i, u_j \rangle\} = b\sum_{ij} m\{\langle u_i, u_j \rangle\}$. Now $m$ is the measure function originally defined on the universe set $U_2 = H_2$, so that $\sum_{ij} m\{\langle u_i, u_j \rangle\} = 1$. Consequently $P(H_2) = b$. By a similar argument, $P(H_1) = a$. But $a + b = 1$. Therefore $P(U^*) = 1$ and axiom (3) is satisfied. It should be noted that the experimental outcome of getting a head followed by a tail is not represented by a simple subset of $U^*$, but by the subset $\{\langle u_1, u_2 \rangle, \langle u_1', u_2' \rangle\}$.

*Bayes' Theorem* seems very promising as a solution to simple inductive inferences involving statistical hypotheses if the notion of assigning an appropriate probability to a hypothesis can be given an objective explication. There are two major ways in which this has been attempted. One way is to regard a hypothesis as a *statement* in a language, and then find the basis for an objective assessment of the probability of a hypothesis in the relationship between it and the other statements which can be formulated in the language (most importantly, the other statements which are known to be true). The other way is to regard a hypothesis as someone's *belief* that the world is correctly described in some way, and to make the probability assignment to the hypothesis one which is compatible with that person's other beliefs under an abstraction of his total belief structure which is made consistent with the help of the probability calculus. The result of the first kind of attempt results in what is commonly called a *logical theory* of probability, and the second kind of attempt results in what is commonly called a *subjective theory* of probability. Both kinds of theories use *Bayes' Theorem* to make inductive inferences on the basis of their assignments of probability

## Bayesian Statistical Inference

measures directly to sets of hypotheses which are taken as partitions of sets of possible experimental results.

Important logical theories have been developed by the philosopher Rudolf Carnap and the statistician Harold Jeffreys. The basis of their assignments of probability measures to hypotheses, however, are quite different.

We have mentioned Carnap's system in a preceding chapter. The intuitive basis of the system is that any given language will only be capable of describing so many *possible worlds*. By assigning measure function values to structures in the language, and subsequently to these possible worlds, probabilities are assigned to hypotheses by summing the measures of the possible worlds in which they would be true. The probability of a hypothesis on *no evidence* (before any experiment has been run) can be defined simply as the probability of the set of structures in which it would be true. Since evidence, so to speak, narrows the range of the possible worlds by excluding some, the probability of a hypothesis, given that evidence, can be defined as the probability assigned to the set of the structures in which the hypothesis would be true if the evidence is true. At any given time, the best estimate of the probability of a hypothesis will be that based on the exclusion of the greatest number of possible worlds by available evidence. This suggestion is incorporated formally by Carnap in his *requirement of total evidence*. Since the probability of general laws is 0 in any language with an infinite domain, Carnap's use of *Bayes' Theorem* in such domains is limited, as was shown earlier.

A logical theory of Carnap's variety is compatible

## Bayesian Statistical Inference

with the objectivistic interpretation of probability. Indeed, Carnap recognizes *two kinds* of probability, the objective probability of certain kinds of events, which he calls *probability$_2$*, and the objective probability of certain statements given the truth of other statements in the same language, which he calls *probability$_1$* and which is defined by his $c(h, e)$ functions. Probability$_1$ statements are the only kind whose truth we can *know* (for certain), and so they may be taken as the *best estimates* available to us of probability$_2$ statements describing the true state of the world. All inductive and predictive reasoning must be carried out in a language in which the relevant probability$_1$ statements can be defined.

Carnap's assignment of probability measures is dependent on a *formalized* language in which the extralogical primitives, etc., can be clearly defined. Jeffreys' attempt at an assignment of probability measures to hypotheses is not dependent on the hypotheses being expressed in a formalized language in this sense. Jeffreys takes mathematics to be the language of science, in that he supposes that every statistical law or hypothesis of a general kind can be represented as a mathematical function. He then attempts to define a consistent simplicity measure function for the forms of all mathematical functions which could be used to abstract scientific hypotheses. For example, he takes any hypothesis which may be expressed as a linear function to be *simpler* than any which cannot be expressed as a linear function but which can be expressed as a non-degenerate quadratic function. He then assigns a probability measure such that those functional forms with the highest simplicity measure are assigned the highest probabilities. The probability of a hypothesis is thus the probability of the simplest functional form in which it can be expressed. The probability of a *form* never changes on any evidence, although the evidence may be incompatible with hypotheses of a simple form. Thus Jeffreys' rule of inductive inference is to prefer that hypothesis compatible with the evidence which may be expressed in the simplest functional form.

The subjective theory has been developed by the philosopher F. P. Ramsey and the statistician L. J. Savage. In the subjective theory, hypotheses are taken as beliefs, and probability measures are assigned to sets of beliefs. Since beliefs are personal, that is they are *some person's* beliefs, the subjective theory does not assign fixed objective or interpersonal probability values to specific hypotheses. The subjective theory allows any person to assign arbitrary values to particular hypotheses based on his subjective degrees of belief in the hypotheses, so long as his total assignment of probability values does not permit the derivation of an incoherency in his total beliefs. The strongest form of incoherency is a derived contradiction resulting from the application of formal probability theory to the values he has assigned. In the subjective theory, one can assign (in the absence of other information) *any* probability value to an arbitrary hypothesis $T$, say $P(T) = p$. But having done this, one must assign the probability value $1 - p$ to any hypothesis which may be abstracted to $-T$ (the denial of $T$) on pain of incoherence. In this case, since the theorem $P(T) + P(-T) = 1$ can be derived in a suitable interpretation of probability theory, any other assignment would entail, along with probability theory, the contradiction that $P(T) + P(-T)$ did and

## Bayesian Statistical Inference

did not have the value $1 - p$. The notion of coherency and the problem of attempting an *objective criterion* of a person's subjective probability estimates is usually clarified by speaking about *betting behaviour*. This gives a criterion of objectivity because coherent beliefs may then be defined as beliefs such that a person cannot engage in a bet consistent with them that will cause him to lose money *no matter what happens*. (Some theorists have proposed even stronger criteria. See [S7].) The problem of identifying a person's subjective probability estimates may then be solved by asking him how he would bet, or observing how he does bet, in certain situations. The subjective theory of probability is not a descriptive theory about how people in fact bet or arrange their beliefs but a normative theory about how people should arrange their beliefs if they wish to be rational. This is quite similar to taking deductive logic, not as a psychological theory about how people in fact reason (since people contradict themselves, and they are likewise often incoherent in their beliefs) but as a tool which a person may use to reason correctly if he consciously wishes to. The objectiveness of the subjective theory does not lie in any claim that different people must *agree* about correct probability estimates (their subjective estimates, and their evidence for making them, may differ) but lies in the claim that a person has strong constraints on his choice of a reasonable overall set of beliefs. The rational person whose beliefs turn out to be incoherent when the various strengths with which they are held are embedded into formal probability theory as probabilities, will revise his beliefs. L. J. Savage has shown that a qualitative ordering of beliefs satisfying certain axioms can be used to define

## Bayesian Statistical Inference

a quantitative probability function, so that the embedding procedure is known to be possible. (See [S3], pp. 30–40.) Because statements about the behaviour of a coin can be regarded as statements of belief about how the coin will behave, the subjective theory is the most ambitious interpretation of the formal theory of probability, holding that a single interpretation (strength of belief) is sufficient for formalizing every reasonably clear occurrence of probability notions both in scientific language and in ordinary speech and thought.

To summarize, the dispute between various shades of opinion which can be regarded as objectivistic or logical or subjectivistic theories of probability is largely a dispute about how a formal theory of probability can successfully be used in scientific investigation. The objectivistic position is the most conservative in that it contends that the mathematical theory of probability can only be used fruitfully to abstract the expected behaviour of an object which shows random properties in repeated trials of some kind. The logical theory may accept the objectivistic theory and argue that a second use of the formal theory can capture the probability of a statement being true on certain evidence in some language, or it may argue that this second use of the formal theory is the only important use. The subjective theory takes the formal theory as a useful device for abstracting the entire structure of anyone's rational beliefs.

One argument advanced by subjectivists to defend their views is interesting for its structural parallels to certain traditional philosophical disputes. It is fairly easy for a subjectivist to show that all actual statistical decisions defended by objectivists are made *as if* the

## Bayesian Statistical Inference

objectivist had made a subjective probability assignment. Consider the coin example of the last chapter. The objectivist chooses between $H_1$ and $H_2$ on the basis of which gives the greatest likelihood to $E$, the experimental outcome. The two instances of *Bayes' Theorem* in this case are the following:

$$P(H_1 \mid E) = \frac{P(H_1)P(E \mid H_1)}{P(H_1)P(E \mid H_1) + P(H_2)P(E \mid H_2)}$$

$$P(H_2 \mid E) = \frac{P(H_2)P(E \mid H_2)}{P(H_1)P(E \mid H_1) + P(H_2)P(E \mid H_2)}$$

Since taking $H_1$ and $H_2$ as equally likely is equivalent to a subjective assignment of $P(H_1) = P(H_2) = 1/2$, and the denominator on the right in both cases is the same, the choice for objectivists is dependent *simply* on whether $P(E \mid H_1)$ or $P(E \mid H_2)$ is greater. The subjectivist thus takes the view that objectivistic statistical inference is but a special case of subjectivistic statistical inference based on *Bayes' Theorem* when the prior probabilities of the alternative hypotheses are taken to be equal. That this does not *prove* any superiority of the subjectivistic view can be seen by comparing it to platonistic–nominalistic disputes in epistemology. Platonists may show that a nominalist always *acts as though* he was acquainted with abstract ideas, but a nominalist is not likely to consider this argument effective unless the platonist can show that his theory of acquaintance with abstract ideas leads to a superior explanation of at least some situations. The subjectivistic argument proves at most that the subjectivistic position is possible, but it is still open to

## Bayesian Statistical Inference

question whether it can prove that it provides decisively superior explanations in at least some contexts.

It cannot even be claimed that *every* objectivistic inference is a special case of subjectivistic inference. The use of *Bayes' Theorem* demands only that the likelihood of the result *actually obtained* as evidence should be calculated on the various hypotheses being considered. Objectivistic inferences sometimes depend on calculating not only the likelihood of the result actually obtained but the likelihood of the various results which *might have been obtained*. But the various results which might have been obtained in a given experiment are a function of experimental design. Suppose that two scientists $A$ and $B$ independently notice that a red-eyed drosophila has appeared among some fruit flies that they have been jointly observing. They wish to determine the frequency with which drosophila have red eyes, and let each of them have 1,000 of the flies at their disposal for testing. Scientist $A$ might decide to take a random sample of 100 flies and count the red-eyed ones. (Random sampling would try to obtain genetically heterogeneous flies to avoid a misleading sample if the eye colour were inheritable in certain ways.) Suppose that 5 flies turn up in 100 with red eyes. Scientist $B$ may feel that $A$'s kind of design may run into the difficulty that *no* red-eyed flies will be observed in the sample, so that one might have to take a new and larger random sample in a new experiment. He may therefore decide to look at flies until he has observed 5 red-eyed flies, and then note the number of flies he had to examine before he found 5 red-eyed. Suppose that the 5th red-eyed fly that he observes is also the 100th fly that he has observed. Then *both* scientists will have observed 5 red-eyed flies

## Bayesian Statistical Inference

in 100 observations of flies. The subjectivist then takes the ratio 5/100 as the evidence for either experiment in calculating the likelihood and he treats the two procedures as equivalent. The objectivist finds that the alternative results to which the given result should be compared are different in the two cases, and he will not feel the same *confidence* in his *estimate* of the frequency of red-eyed flies following the one procedure rather than the other, even though the estimates themselves are the same. In our example, the objectivist calculating 5% frequency on the second procedure would feel more confident that he had found the correct ratio than the objectivist calculating 5% on the first procedure. Subjectivists hold that one should feel equally confident in the correctness of the estimate (5%) on both procedures, since the statistic representing the observed ratio and the calculated likelihood will lead to the same inferences.

Conflict between views disappears as sample size increases. Thus, if enough flies are observed in the two objectivistic procedures and the same ratio of red-eyed flies is observed in each, the confidence in the estimates based on the two procedures will gradually coincide. A philosopher accepting the logical definition of probability (depending on whether or not he accepts *two* legitimate uses of the formal calculus) may side with either objectivists or subjectivists on these matters. All three views gradually coincide in recommending the same inferences with the same level of confidence under the weight of increasing evidence, and in this sense they are all empirical theories whose rules satisfy the criterion of sensitivity to evidence. Their differences appear largely in the examination of relatively small samples as evidence, an area in which

## Bayesian Statistical Inference

it is difficult to decide between them because of the difficulty in resolving conflicting inferences in simple cases by an appeal to expected success.

There is a rather interesting attempt at a compromise between subjectivistic and objectivistic theories in the newly developing *empirical Bayes approach*. This approach is to use past empirical evidence for estimating probability distributions for the alternative hypotheses being considered in some statistical inference, the estimated distribution being in turn tested by new empirical evidence. An insight leading to this approach is that past probability estimates may be the best guides for choosing experimental designs, while the results obtained from running the experiments are best interpreted solely in terms of likelihood ratios. In this approach, different problems are discerned in designing and then interpreting experiments. These suggestions are introducing considerable ferment into foundational studies in statistics at the present time.

### Further Reading

An interesting introduction to the differences in approach to practical statistical problems made by objectivists and subjectivists may be found in [A2]. [B6], [C8], [F1], [F3], [N2], [N3], [N4], [P2], [R3], [R4], and [W1] are written from an objectivist point of view. [B2], [B3], [G2], [L5], [R2], [S3], [S4], [S5], and [S9] are by subjectivists, and [K4] is an anthology of important subjectivists' papers. Logical views are developed in [C2], [C3], and [J1]. [G2], pp. 6–12 contains an interesting classification of various theories of probability along somewhat different lines than those used in this chapter Small sample differences between

## Bayesian Statistical Inference

objectivists and subjectivists are discussed in [B2] and [S5]. Probabilities pertinent to the example of the red-eyed flies are given in [B2]. Attempts to use features of both objectivistic and subjectivistic theories in empirical Bayes methods are found in [H1], [N4], and [R4].

## Chapter Six

# STATISTICAL DECISION AND UTILITY

In statistical inference, one is concerned with deciding what hypothesis in some set of hypotheses is most reasonable given certain evidence. If maximum likelihood estimates seem appropriate, then the result of statistical inference is to select that hypothesis on which the likelihood of the evidence is greatest, or if there is more than one hypothesis with maximum likelihood in this sense, one from among them. The curious fact is that it does not always seem rational to act *as though* the hypothesis that is selected by statistical inference is in fact most reasonable. This can be demonstrated by simple examples. It may seem more likely to Dan that his wallet is empty than that it has £5 in it, and yet Dan may *look into it anyway* if he needs £5 on the grounds that he cannot lose anything by looking. This may assume that the time that he spends looking does not really matter to him, in that there is no alternative line of action that gives any more promise of producing £5. If Dan acted on the hypothesis that his pocket was empty, he would not look into it in the hopes of finding £5. Now let the example be changed slightly. Suppose that Dan has £1 and Bob has £4. Suppose further that neither of them has prospects for ready cash beyond these amounts in the immediate future but that they both want very badly to do something that would cost £5. They might decide to take the following gamble. A die that both of them consider fair is to be tossed once by a means that they both consider to produce an unpredictable result. If the die shows 1 spot after the toss, Bob turns £4 over to Dan, and if any other number of spots shows uppermost, Dan hands over his pound to Bob. This bet is not reasonable in an abstract sense, since if the die is fair and the tossing procedure random, if Dan were to make an equivalent bet over and over when he had a pound to bet, he would slowly lose pounds. Yet the possibility (even though it is small) of achieving a greatly desired goal may lead him to incur an expectation of immediate loss in order to achieve it. This kind of situation presents itself over and over in ordinary life, and it seems equally inescapable in scientific research. The general problem is this: one is faced with a number of possible courses of action which will turn out to have certain kinds of desirable or undesirable outcomes depending on which of several unknown states of the universe actually obtains, and he must make a choice of action in this situation. The gambling situation for Dan could be formalized as in Fig. 8.

This abstraction depends on several features that should be explicitly noted. The possible acts are such that one of them will be performed. Due to philosophical difficulties with the notion of an act, it may seem inappropriate to call *not gambling* an act, so it may be preferable to say that the *acts* are really claims about

*Statistical Decision and Utility*

|  |  | Possible states if die is tossed | |
|---|---|---|---|
|  |  | Die shows 1 | Die does not show 1 |
| Possible Acts | gamble | Have £5 | Have £0 |
|  | don't gamble | Have £1 | Have £1 |

Fig. 8

the expected behaviour of the agent one of which will be *true of* the action that he takes. Further, it is supposed in this abstraction that the agent *knows* the *outcomes* of his acts under the various states which may obtain. This supposition is actually quite strong, and can only be more or less well approximated in practical examples. For example, abstraction may be false on the example situation because unknown to Bob, if the two parties gamble and the 1 spot fails to turn up, the loser may cosh the winner and have £5 anyway. Further, it is assumed that the states are such that at least one, and only one, will obtain. The assumption that the outcomes are known will be the background for the introduction of a probability measure over these states. The problem for the agent in these situations is to decide what to do when the state of affairs, and consequently the outcome of his action, is uncertain. The problem of decision making under uncertainty has played a very important role in the contemporary study of nondeductive inference. In general, decision making embraces the problem of deciding what to do when one has successfully solved a problem of nondeductive inference.

A formal decision making problem has three elements, a set of *acts*, a set of possible *outcomes*, and a

## Statistical Decision and Utility

set of *states* which correlate the outcomes to the acts. In more mathematical treatments, it is usually convenient to consider acts as functions from the set of states to the set of outcomes. (See [S3], pp. 13–17.) Thus in the decision making problem represented above, the act *gamble* could be represented by the function $f$ so defined that:

$$f(1) = \text{Have £5},$$
$$f(\sim 1) = \text{Have £0}.$$

The act *don't gamble* could be represented by the function $g$ so defined that:

$$g(1) = \text{Have £1},$$
$$g(\sim 1) = \text{Have £1}.$$

At this point there is not enough information available to lead to a reasonable decision between the two acts. Now let a probability function be assigned over the set of *states*. In the example, $P(1) = 1/6$ and $P(\sim 1) = 5/6$ seems to be the appropriate probability function. When this is assigned, the decision making situation is determinate enough for choice. It is not known exactly which state will occur, but we know the probability with which each state will occur. These probabilities enable us to calculate an aggregate expected income for each act as follows. Act 1 (*gamble*) will result in £5 with a probability of 1/6, and in £0 with a probability of 5/6. The aggregate expected outcome of act 1 is thus taken as the sum of the possible outcomes on each state times the probability of that state. For act 1, this is $(1/6 \times 5) + (5/6 \times 0)$ or 5/6 of a pound. In other words, if act 1 were repeated under similar circumstances enough times, one would expect to average 5/6 of a pound from all such

## Statistical Decision and Utility

bets. The aggregate expected outcome of act 2 (*don't gamble*) is $(1/6 \times 1) + (5/6 \times 1)$ or £1. (This, of course, is trivial, since under the conditions of the problem, not gambling is to result in retention of the original pound.) In any given gamble Dan does not receive 5/6 of a pound, but loses a pound or gains £4, depending on the particular state that obtains. From the present abstraction of the problem, the act of gambling does not appear to be a very wise choice, since it amounts to losing (on the average) 1/6 of a pound.

But the original problem seemed quite genuine, and the circumstances might be such that the outcome of spending the £5 (a ticket to the FA Cup Final) might be so attractive that Dan would be willing to take a theoretically 'unfair' bet in order to have a chance of achieving it. What Dan seems to be doing in such a situation is not measuring the outcome of the wager *merely* in pounds but in terms of the desirability of the various outcomes. Only a fictional capitalist would act solely to increase his wealth. The previous abstraction is misleading just because Dan may prefer owning a ticket to the Cup Final to owning £5. Let us symbolize this preference by the following ordering: £5 < ticket to the Cup Final. Now let the previous problem be abstracted in this way:

|                      | $S_1$<br>1           | $S_2$<br>$-1$   |
| -------------------- | -------------------- | --------------- |
| Act 1<br>(*gamble*)  | Cup Final<br>ticket  | Disappointment  |
| Act 2<br>(*don't gamble*) | £1              | £1              |

Fig. 9

## Statistical Decision and Utility

Now the difficulty is that Dan cannot compute an aggregate expected outcome for both acts on this basis because the sum (1/6 Cup Final ticket + 5/6 disappointment) does not result in a quantity of anything. Yet Dan may feel that he can order the various outcomes in terms of their desirability as follows:

disappointment < £1 < £5 < Cup Final ticket.

What kind of an ordering is this? Many logicians and statisticians have called such an ordering of preferences or desirability a *utility* ordering. The simplest kind of utility ordering is one in which preferences are simply ranked into the order in which someone would prefer them. Now there may be outcomes that one cannot choose between in certain situations. It may happen, for example, that one cannot decide between two different sweet rolls at breakfast (where only one can be eaten due to family democracy). If one is truly indifferent, he might be said to prefer them equally, so that they would both occur in the same place on his utility ordering. We could extend our probability background to hold that one prefers $A$ and $B$ equally if he does not care which he receives when a coin he believes fair is tossed to decide between them. We often say that we flip a 'mental coin' to decide such situations.

The next interesting question to consider is whether a simple utility ordering can be extended to a utility scale. Many logicians and statisticians have thought that a rational person could extend his preference orderings to a utility *scale* that is implicit in his orderings by considering bets that he would be willing to take or to give which would have his preferences as outcomes. The property that such a preference scale measures is called *utility*, and the ordering considered

## Statistical Decision and Utility

earlier can be considered a simple utility ranking. The utility property is abstracted out of felt preferences in a manner analogous to the way that the temperature property was abstracted out of felt differences of warm and cold. Temperatures are measured by *degrees* in a temperature scale, and numbers of *utiles* can be similarly used to define utility scales that capture the relative strength and the ordering of someone's preferences in a given situation. In our example, an abstracted utility scale would assign a greater number of utiles to the Cup Final ticket than to the possession of £5 to indicate the fact that the ticket is definitely preferred to the money, even though the decision situation is such that Dan can only win the money which must in turn be converted into the desired ticket.

Suppose that 1 utile is assigned to the possession of £1 in these circumstances, 0 utiles to the possession of £0, and 7 utiles to the possession of £5 because it is equivalent to obtaining the Cup Final ticket. Then the situation may be abstracted with *utiles* as outcomes in the following manner:

|       | $S_1$ | $S_2$ |
|-------|-------|-------|
|       | 1     | −1    |
| Act 1 | 7     | 0     |
| Act 2 | 1     | 1     |

Fig. 10

Now the aggregate expected outcome of act 1 is $(1/6 \times 7) + (5/6 \times 0)$ or 1 1/6 utiles, while the aggregate expected outcome of act 2 is $(1/6 \times 1) + (5/6 \times 1)$ or 1 utile. With the outcomes expressed in utiles, the act of gambling now appears to be the reasonable alternative.

## *Statistical Decision and Utility*

There may seem to be something arbitrary about the idea of assigning utiles to indicate the strength of a person's preferences for various outcomes, but although it is a relatively recent idea, it is an instance of a technique of abstraction that has proved quite valuable in scientific history. It may be compared in this respect to the abstraction of temperature scales. Before temperature scales were introduced, objects could often be ranked according to their warmth by simple observation. From these observations it is easy to hypostatize a property (temperature) of any object that would represent its place in such rankings. It is not necessary to sketch the various methods of attempting to find a measure of this property. One important method followed from the observation that mercury continuously expands with increasing temperature. By putting some mercury in a small tube under low pressure, its expansion could easily be measured as the length of the mercury column in the tube. Then by fixing some points of measurement, say the place where the mercury is when water freezes and the place it is when it boils, one marks off in equal lengths some scale of degrees on the glass tube to represent temperatures which are in between those at the two fixed points as well as temperatures which may be extrapolated beyond them. We can suppose that the divisions are marked by consecutive integers indicating the number of degrees, by convention letting the integers increase between the freezing and boiling points of water. It is well known that such a scale is arbitrary in that various scales can be used for the purpose. The Fahrenheit and Centigrade scales are both commonly used for this purpose. However, it can be proved that any two scales marked off in this fashion

## Statistical Decision and Utility

bear a simple mathematical relationship to each other. If $x$ stands for the number abstracting degrees of temperature on one such scale, then the number abstracting degrees of temperature for the same temperature on the other scale will be related to it by some instance of the equation '$f(x) = ax + b$', where $f(x)$ is the number of degrees on the second scale, and $a$ and $b$ ($a > 0$) are fixed parameters. For Centigrade and Fahrenheit temperature scales, for example, if $x$ is the number of degrees assigned to some temperature on the Centigrade scale, then $f(x)$, the number of degrees assigned to that temperature on the Fahrenheit scale will be '$9/5\ x + 32$'. Here $a = 9/5$ and $b = 32$. Any other choice of $a$ and $b$ ($a > 0$) as values for the parameters in the equation would also define a temperature scale that would be mathematically equivalent to the Centigrade scale for the purpose of abstracting a temperature scale. This may be put formally by saying that all suitable temperature scales are linearly related to each other.

The abstraction of a utility scale is mathematically quite similar. The fact that any class of outcomes can seemingly be ranked according to preferences suggests that there is some property of any outcome (its utility) that might be measured by constructing a utility scale. By measuring the relative preference of other outcomes by means of the bets that we would take on the various outcomes, we can fix a utility scale for our preferences about outcomes. Any such scale that has been fixed is equivalent mathematically for its purpose to any scale related to it by the same kind of transformation that characterized temperature scales. If $x$ is the number of utiles assigned to an outcome on one suitable utility ranking, then the

## Statistical Decision and Utility

ranking defined by the equation '$f(x) = ax + b$' for fixed $a$ ($a > 0$) and $b$ will assign an appropriate number of utiles to that outcome in a preference ranking mathematically equivalent to the first. To say that they are mathematically equivalent in this context means that either utility scale would lead to the same choice of action in a decision problem where the acts and states are such that the relative preferences of the outcomes may be suitably expressed by either ranking.

We can easily see that such a transformation will preserve the properties required of a utility ranking. First, if $A$ and $B$ are two possible outcomes, and $A$ is preferred to $B$, then $B < A$ in the utility ranking. If $u(A)$ and $u(B)$ assign some number of utiles to $A$ and $B$, then $u(B) < u(A)$ in an appropriate utility scale. Let $u(A)$ and $u(B)$ both be multiplied by some positive number $a$ ($a > 0$). The inequality will still hold. Let some positive number be added to $u(A)$ and $u(B)$. The inequality will still hold. Thus if we take the number of utiles assigned to each outcome on one appropriate utility ranking, any new utility ranking obtained by multiplying the number of utiles assigned on the original ranking by a positive number and adding some fixed number to each of these results will preserve the ordering of preferences represented by the first ranking. The other property required of a utility ranking is that the number of utiles assigned to the outcomes must reflect our (potential and actual) betting behaviour. But if the chance of gaining outcome $A$ with probability $p_1$ is preferred to the chance of gaining outcome $B$ with probability $p_2$, i.e. the scale is such that $p_2(u(B)) < p_1(u(A))$, then by a similar argument it can be shown that this ranking will be preserved by the same kind of transformation.

## Statistical Decision and Utility

There is, of course, an important difference between temperature and utility scales. Where the freezing point of water is an objective criterion by which various temperature rankings can be compared, no similar objective criterion is available for the intercomparison of utility rankings. For any two possible outcomes, it seems conceivable that some will prefer one of them to the other, but that some person would reverse this preference in his own utility ranking. This fact makes any interpersonal comparison of utility rankings extremely difficult.

In ordinary decision problems, it is not always necessary to change the outcomes to utiles, since all of the outcomes may be expressed in terms of numbers of some unit which can be taken as a very near approximation to the numbers of utiles which could be assigned in a satisfactory utility scale. For example, if one is trying to choose a course of action after having *accepted* some gambling situation, then all of the outcomes will already be expressed in numbers of some money unit. Amounts of money will function as a reasonable approximation to numbers of utiles in typical gambling situations (where the money is not seen as a means to some end, as in the Cup Final ticket gamble between Dan and Bob), particularly where the possible money outcomes are all small in relations to the gamblers' total wealth. It is easy to see that money units and utiles are not always approximate equivalents, since a man whose total wealth is £10 will (in typical cases) regard an increase in his wealth of £1 as having more utiles than will a man whose total wealth is £1,000,000. Similarly, if a person accepts the playing of some game with an opponent, all of the outcomes may be either *win* or *lose*. In this case, the

## Statistical Decision and Utility

assessment of acts is directly related to the probability that they will produce a *win* for the player. As these examples illustrate, the study of *game theory* in the modern sense is closely related to the general problem of decision making under uncertainty.

We can now discuss *strategies* that can be employed to solve decision making problems. There are three strategies which have been widely discussed for the generalized decision problem: the maximization of expected utility strategy (hereafter referred to as the MEU strategy); the minimization of maximum expected risk strategy (hereafter referred to as the *minimax risk* strategy); and the minimization of maximum expected regret strategy (hereafter referred to as the *minimax regret* strategy).

The MEU strategy is the strategy that was implicitly used in the discussion of the gambling problem. The MEU strategy is simply to calculate for each act the *expected utility* of the act by summing the product of the probability of a state by the utility of the outcome of the act for that state over every state. Thus, if $S_1, \ldots, S_n$ are the states, and $U_1, \ldots, U_n$ are the utiles assigned to the outcome on each state for an act 1, then the expected utility of act 1 is:

$$EU_1 = \sum_{i=1}^{n} P(S_1) \times U_i.$$

The MEU strategy is to select the act whose expected utility is greatest, or one of the acts whose expected utility is greatest if there are more than one. Use of the MEU strategy depends upon a probability distribution assigned over the possible states of a decision problem. Consequently, the MEU strategy is usually adopted for solving decision problems by those who

## Statistical Decision and Utility

accept the logical or subjective theories of probability, since their probability techniques can supply a probability measure for the set of states.

Objectivists in probability theory cannot usually accept a probability measure over the set of states, although when they can, the MEU strategy is satisfactory to them. When no probability measure over the states is available, the objectivist acts as though *any* probability distribution might be the right one. The intuition of objectivists in such situations is to adopt very cautious strategies that minimize the chance of obtaining undesirable results.

Assume that all of the utiles assigned to various outcomes in some decision problem are positive integers. Now the *risk* of taking any act, given that any state might be the true state, is that of losing the number of utiles expressing one's relative preference for an outcome if it obtains. In other words, what one stands to gain in utility if things work out favourably is what one risks losing if things work out unfavourably. Thus *risk* might be abstracted as *negative utility*. If $u(A)$ is the number of utiles assigned to outcome $A$ in some utility ranking, $-u(A)$ represents the risk with respect to that outcome in the choice situation. Let any choice matrix be converted to a risk matrix by replacing the number of utiles assigned to various outcomes by the negative number of utiles. For the example above, the *risk* matrix is:

|  | $S_1$ | $S_2$ |
|---|---|---|
|  | 1 | −1 |
| Act 1 | −7 | 0 |
| Act 2 | −1 | −1 |

Fig. 11

## Statistical Decision and Utility

Minimax risk strategy is to minimize the maximum risk. For each act, one calculates the maximum risk involved in that act. In the example, the maximum risk of act 1 is $-7$ and the maximum risk of act 2 is $-1$. One then chooses to act so as to minimize the maximum risk. The minimax risk strategy chooses act 2, quite different advice from the MEU strategy. The minimax risk strategy, in effect, counsels action on the assumption that the worst may well happen.

Minimax regret strategies are also cautious. *Regret* is defined as the difference between the outcome actually obtained when some act is chosen, and the outcome that might have been obtained by some act under the most favourable circumstances. A matrix containing the number of utiles assigned to every outcome given an act, is converted to a regret matrix by entering for each outcome the (positive) difference between the number of utiles assigned to that outcome, and the maximum number of utiles assigned to some outcome on the same state of nature by some act. The regret matrix for the example is:

|       | $S_1$ | $S_2$ |
|-------|-------|-------|
|       | 1     | $-1$  |
| Act 1 | 0     | 1     |
| Act 2 | 6     | 0     |

Fig. 12

The minimax regret strategy is then to apply the minimax risk strategy to the regret matrix of a choice situation. In the case of the example, the risk matrix of the regret matrix is:

*Statistical Decision and Utility*

|       | $S_1$ | $S_2$ |
|-------|-------|-------|
|       | 1     | −1    |
| Act 1 | 0     | −1    |
| Act 2 | −6    | 0     |

Fig. 13

The maximum risk for act 1 is −1 utile and for act 2 it is −6 utiles. The minimax regret strategy is thus equivalent to the MEU strategy for our example.

It is not difficult to find choice situations in which the three strategies differ. A choice situation might be abstracted to the following matrix:

|       | $S_1$ | $S_2$ | $S_3$ | $S_4$ |
|-------|-------|-------|-------|-------|
| Act 1 | 2     | 2     | 0     | 1     |
| Act 2 | 1     | 1     | 1     | 1     |
| Act 3 | 0     | 4     | 0     | 0     |
| Act 4 | 1     | 3     | 0     | 0     |

Fig. 14

By constructing the appropriate regret and risk matrices, it can easily be seen that act 1 would be chosen by the MEU strategy under a very wide range of possible assignments of probability measures to the possible states (such as the one in which they are all taken to be equally likely), act 2 by the minimax risk strategy, and act 4 by the minimax regret strategy. (This matrix and the computation for it are given in [M2].)

The MEU strategy cannot be employed where an assignment of a probability measure to the possible states is not possible. As we have seen, objectivists cannot use the MEU strategy in a wide range of decision problems. Going back to our earlier example, if a stranger pulled a die out of his pocket and offered a bet on the Cup Final ticket, an objectivist would have to refuse the bet because no probability assignment for the die could be given. But there are difficulties for a subjectivist as well. After throwing the die a few times, he may be able to frame an estimate of the probability distribution that only lies within various limits. In other words, his evidence may be such that he does not believe that a specific probability distribution is the correct one but only that the distribution is one among several. Faced with a difficult decision to be based on the toss of the die, calculation of MEU strategies for the various possible distributions may select different acts from among those which are available to him. The general problem of a *best strategy* for an arbitrary decision problem is thus not solved by any simple consideration of the three strategies that have been cited. An attempt to locate very general strategies for solving decision problems where exact probability distributions cannot be employed is thus a nondeductive problem of considerable importance.

**Further Reading**

Lucid introductory accounts of decision problems and strategies may be found in [C6], [L6], and [S4]. Many problems of statistical inference can be illuminatingly considered as special cases of decision problems. This approach is implicit in [B5] and [S4]. Discussions of strategies and useful bibliographies will be found in [C5], [F4], [L6], and [T1].

## Chapter Seven

# THEORIES AND RATIONALITY

We bring this monograph to a close with a brief description of some further nondeductive problems which are the focus of continuing controversy in the philosophy of science, and with a brief reminder of the important bearing of nondeductive inference on traditional problems of philosophy.

The simple inductive problems discussed in this monograph have all been restricted to those which can be formulated in terms of properties *common* to the evidence and the alternative hypotheses. Some properties ascribed to individuals in the evidence have been used, along with logical and mathematical vocabulary, to formulate generalizations or statistical hypotheses equivalent to the hypotheses to be chosen between in the problems. In addition, the order in which the observations reported in the evidence were taken has been assumed to be of no significance. If the alternative hypotheses in a statistical problem are scientific theories mentioning theoretical properties not ascribed to the examined individuals, however, the first restriction and often the second need to be relaxed.

Let a simple inductive problem involving alternative

## *Theories and Rationality*

theories be given, and let us assume that the theories are both *confirmed* by the evidence, that is, that the evidence (within an acceptable range of experimental error) is what both theories ascribe to the examined individuals. For example, let four observations of $A$'s be made, and let it be discovered that 3/4 of all the examined $A$'s are $B$'s. Now let two theories $M$ and $N$ be postulated. Let $M$ be such that one can deduce from it that every other $A$ in a certain series is not a $B$, and let $N$ be such that one can deduce from it that every third $A$ in a similar series is not a $B$. If we let 1, 2, 3, ... represent places in the relevant series, $M$ and $N$ may describe the following:

```
    1     2     3      4     5     6      7     8
M  A.B  A.-B  A.B    A.-B  A.B  A.-B    A.B  A.-B
N  A.B  A.B   A.-B   A.B   A.B  A.-B    A.B  A.B
```

Now if we then observe that our evidence could consist of observations of places 1, 5, 6, 7 in either of these series, the evidence would support both $M$ and $N$. But it is clear that quite incompatible predictions are to be made from the two theories, and we should not want to accept both on the basis of an inductive inference.

This situation is quite common in the sciences. The obvious answer in the case of $M$ and $N$ is to suspend judgment until some members of the series where $M$ and $N$ conflict are observed in order to choose between them. But it is often the case in scientific history that all known evidence and all immediately expected evidence is such that either of the two theories is compatible with it, and yet the theories make some conflicting claims about some (at least as yet) unobservable events. In such cases, criteria other than the

## Theories and Rationality

nature of the evidence must be invoked if a choice is to be made that one of the two is more reasonable than the other. The criteria usually invoked are *simplicity* (the simpler hypothesis is more acceptable) and *cost of acceptance* (the hypothesis whose adoption entails least revision in what we already accept is more acceptable). A criterion of choice between arbitrary theories compatible with available evidence may well turn out to be some subtle blend of both. But the role of theories and the proposed measures of simplicity and cost of acceptance raise subtle issues in the philosophy of science that take us beyond the compass of this monograph.

The importance of nondeductive inference is easily illustrated by its close connection with traditional philosophical investigations of rationality. A rational man cannot believe only what is not capable of being false (logical truths). He must commit himself to the truth of at least some observations, and in this commitment he is no doubt correctly influenced by the observational reports of others. We should also expect that he will continue to accept as true any new observations (implicitly or explicitly) satisfying certain epistemological criteria. Rationality, then, seems to consist in apportioning one's strength of belief in certain hypotheses according to their reasonableness on this evidence. The mark of irrationality is to maintain a high strength of belief in some favourite hypothesis in spite of conflicting evidence, and the mark, perhaps, of common human failing is to allow our favourite hypotheses greater strength of belief than certain others no better supported by the evidence. The relevance of nondeductive inference to the apportionment of strengths of belief is obvious. It may be

## *Theories and Rationality*

the mark of genius to frame new hypotheses not previously considered by human beings. But a man can be rational without being a genius, and, indeed, various men may have quite different sets of hypotheses to bring into harmony with the evidence available to them as a result of native intelligence or education.

# BIBLIOGRAPHY

[A1] ACHINSTEIN, PETER. See [B1].
[A2] ANSCOMBE, F. J. 'Bayesian Statistics." *The American Statistician*, **15** (1961), pp. 21–24.
[B1] BARKER, STEPHEN, and ACHINSTEIN, PETER. 'On the New Riddle of Induction.' *The Philosophical Review*, **69** (1960), pp. 511–522.
[B2] BARNARD, G. A., JENKINS, G. M., and WINSTEN, C. B. 'Likelihood Inference and Time Series.' *Journal of the Royal Statistical Society*, series A, **125** (1962), pp. 321–372.
[B3] BIRNBAUM, ALLAN. 'On the Foundations of Statistical Inference.' *Journal of the American Statistical Association*, **57** (1962), pp. 269–326.
[B4] BRAITHWAITE, R. B. 'Probability and Induction.' Pp. 133–151 of Mace, C. A. (ed.), *British Philosophy in the Mid-Century*, London, 1957.
[B5] BRAITHWAITE, R. B. 'The Role of Values in Scientific Inference.' Pp. 180–204 of Kyburg, H. E., and Nagel, E. (eds.), *Induction; Some Current Issues*, Middletown, 1963.
[B6] BRAITHWAITE, R. B. *Scientific Explanation*. Cambridge, 1955.
[B7] BROSS, I. D. J. 'Statistical Dogma: A Challenge.' *The American Statistician*, **15** (1961), pp. 14–15.
[B8] BURKS, A. W. 'On the Presuppositions of Induction.' *Review of Metaphysics*, **8** (1954–55), pp. 574–611.

## Bibliography

[C1] CARNAP, RUDOLF. *The Continuum of Inductive Methods.* Chicago, 1952.

[C2] CARNAP, RUDOLF. *Logical Foundations of Probability.* (2nd edn.) Chicago, 1962.

[C3] CARNAP, RUDOLF. 'Replies and Systematic Expositions.' Pp. 859–1017 of Schilpp, P. A. (ed.), *The Philosophy of Rudolf Carnap*, LaSalle, 1963.

[C4] CARNAP, RUDOLF. 'Reply to Nelson Goodman.' *Philosophy and Phenomenological Research*, **8** (1947), pp. 461–462.

[C5] CHERNOFF, HERMANN. 'Rational Selection of Decision Functions.' *Econometrica*, **22** (1954), pp. 422–443.

[C6] CHERNOFF, HERMANN, and MOSES, LINCOLN. *Elementary Decision Theory.* New York, 1959.

[C7] COOMBS, C. H. See [T1].

[C8] CRAMER, HARALD. *Mathematical Methods of Statistics.* Princeton, 1951.

[F1] FELLER, W. *An Introduction to Probability Theory and Its Applications.* Vol. I. New York, 1950.

[F2] FISHER, R. A. *Statistical Methods and Scientific Inference.* London, 1956.

[F3] FISHER, R. A. *Statistical Methods for Research Workers.* Edinburgh and London, 1925.

[F4] FRIEDMAN, MILTON, and SAVAGE, L. J. 'The Utility Analysis of Choices Involving Risk.' *The Journal of Political Economy*, **56** (1948), pp. 279–304.

[G1] GOOD, I. J. 'The Paradox of Confirmation,' Parts I and II, *British Journal for the Philosophy of Science*, **11** (1960), pp. 145–148, and **12** (1961), pp. 63–64.

[G2] GOOD, I. J. *Probability and the Weighing of Evidence.* London, 1950.

## Bibliography

[G3] GOODMAN, NELSON. *Fact, Fiction, and Forecast.* Cambridge, 1955.

[G4] GOODMAN, NELSON. 'On Infirmities of Confirmation Theory.' *Philosophy and Phenomenological Research*, **8** (1947), pp. 149–151.

[G5] GOODMAN, NELSON. 'Positionality and Pictures.' *Philosophical Review*, **69** (1960), pp. 523–525.

[G6] GOODMAN, NELSON. 'A Query on Confirmation.' *Journal of Philosophy*, **43** (1946), pp. 383–385.

[H1] HACKING, IAN. 'On the Foundations of Statistics.' *British Journal for the Philosophy of Science*, **15** (1964), pp. 1–26.

[H2] HEMPEL, CARL G. 'Studies in the Logic of Confirmation.' *Mind*, **54** (1945), pp. 1–26, 97–121.

[H3] HOEL, PAUL G. *Introduction to Mathematical Statistics.* (3rd edn.) New York, 1962.

[H4] HODGES, J. L., JR., and LEHMANN, E. L. 'The Use of Previous Experience in Reaching Statistical Decisions.' *Annals of Mathematical Statistics*, **23** (1952), pp. 396–407.

[J1] JEFFREYS, HAROLD. *Theory of Probability.* (3rd edn.) Oxford, 1961.

[J2] JENKINS, G. M. See [B2].

[K1] KEMENY, JOHN G. 'Carnap's Theory of Probability and Induction.' Pp. 711–739 of Schilpp, P. A. (ed.), *The Philosophy of Rudolf Carnap*, LaSalle, 1963.

[K2] KYBURG, H. E. 'Recent Work in Inductive Logic.' *American Philosophical Quarterly*, **1** (1964), pp. 249–287.

[K3] KYBURG, H. E., and NAGEL, ERNEST (eds.). *Induction; Some Current Issues.* Middletown, 1963.

[K4] KYBURG, H. E., and SMOKLER, H. E. (eds.).

*Studies in Subjective Probability.* New York, 1964.

[L1] LEBLANC, HUGUES. 'A Revised Version of Goodman's Paradox on Confirmation.' *Philosophical Studies*, 14 (1963), pp. 49–51.

[L2] LEHMANN, E. L. 'Some Principles of the Theory of Testing Hypotheses.' *Annals of Mathematical Statistics*, 21 (1950), pp. 1–26.

[L3] LEHMANN, E. L. See [H4].

[L4 LINDLEY, D. V. 'Professor Hogben's "Crisis"—A Survey of the Foundations of Statistics.' *Applied Statistics*, 7 (1958), pp. 186–198.

[L5] LINDLEY, D. V. 'Statistical Inference.' *Journal of the Royal Statistical Society*, series *B*, 17 (1953), pp. 30–65.

[L6] LUCE, R. D., and RAIFFA, H. *Games and Decisions.* New York, 1957.

[M1] MACKIE, J. L. 'The Paradox of Confirmation.' *British Journal for the Philosophy of Science*, 13 (1962–63), pp. 265–277.

[M2] MILNOR, JOHN. 'Games Against Nature.' Pp. 49–60 of Thrall, R. M., Coombs, C. H., and Davis, R. L. (eds.), *Decision Processes*, New York, 1954.

[M3] MOSES, LINCOLN. See [C6].

[M4] MORGENBESSER, S. 'Goodman on the Ravens.' *Journal of Philosophy*, 59 (1962), pp. 493–495.

[N1] NAGEL, ERNEST. See [K3].

[N2] NEYMAN, J. *A First Course in Probability and Statistics.* New York, 1950.

[N3] NEYMAN, J. ' "Inductive Behaviour" As a Basic Concept of Philosophy of Science.' *Revue De L'Institut International De Statistique*, 24 (1956), pp. 7–22.

*Bibliography*

[N4] NEYMAN, J. 'Two Breakthroughs in the Theory of Statistical Decision Making.' *Revue De L'Institut International De Statistique*, **30** (1962), pp. 11–27.

[P1] PITT, H. R. *Integration, Measure, and Probability.* London, 1963.

[P2] POPPER, K. R. *The Logic of Scientific Discovery.* London, 1959.

[Q1] QUENOUILLE, M. H. *Fundamentals of Statistical Reasoning.* London, 1958.

[R1] RAIFFA, H. See [L6].

[R2] RAMSEY, F. P. 'Truth and Probability.' Reprinted in Braithwaite, R. B. (ed.), *The Foundations of Mathematics and Other Logical Essays by F. P. Ramsey*, New York, 1950. Also reprinted in [K4].

[R3] REICHENBACH, HANS. *The Theory of Probability.* Los Angeles, 1949.

[R4] ROBBINS, HERBERT. 'A New Approach to a Classical Decision Problem.' Pp. 101–114 of Kyburg, H. E., and Nagel, Ernest (eds.), *Induction: Some Current Issues*, Middletown, 1963.

[R5] RUDNER, RICHARD S. 'The Scientist Qua Scientist Makes Value Judgments.' *Philosophy of Science*, **20** (1953), pp. 1–6.

[S1] SALMON, WESLEY. 'On Vindicating Induction.' Pp. 27–41 of Kyburg, H. E., and Nagel, Ernest (eds.), *Induction; Some Current Issues*, Middletown, 1963.

[S2] SALMON, WESLEY. 'Vindication of Induction.' Pp. 245–257 of Feigl, H., and Maxwell, G. (eds.), *Current Issues in the Philosophy of Science*, New York, 1961.

*Bibliography*

[S3] SAVAGE, L. J. *The Foundations of Statistics*. New York, 1954.
[S4] SAVAGE, L. J. 'The Theory of Statistical Decision.' *Journal of the American Statistical Association*, 46 (1951), pp. 55–67.
[S5] SAVAGE, L. J., and others. *The Foundations of Statistical Inference*. London, 1962.
[S6] SCHEFFLER, ISRAEL. *The Anatomy of Inquiry*. New York, 1963.
[S7] SCHICK, F. 'Rationality and Consistency.' *Journal of Philosophy*, 60 (1963), pp. 5–19.
[S8] SCHILPP, P. A. (ed.). *The Philosophy of Rudolf Carnap*. LaSalle, 1963.
[S9] SMITH, C. A. B. 'Consistency in Statistical Inference and Decision.' *Journal of the Royal Statistical Society*, series B, 23 (1961), pp. 1–37.
[S10] SMOKLER, H. E. See [K4].
[S11] STUART, ALAN. *Basic Ideas of Scientific Sampling*. London, 1962.
[S12] SUPPES, PATRICK. *Introduction to Logic*. New York, 1957.
[T1] THRALL, R. M., COOMBS, C. H., and DAVIS, R. L. (eds.). *Decision Processes*. New York, 1954.
[U1] ULLIAN, JOSEPH. 'More on "Grue" and Grue.' *Philosophical Review*, 70 (1961), pp. 731–738.
[W1] WALD, ABRAHAM. *On the Principles of Statistical Inference*. Notre Dame, 1952.
[W2] WALD, ABRAHAM. *Statistical Decision Functions*. New York, 1950.
[W3] WILL, F. L. 'Justification and Induction.' *Philosophical Review*, 68 (1959), pp. 359–372
[W4] WINSTEN, C. B. See [B2].

## INDEX OF DEFINITIONS

ADDITION Theorem, 45

Bayes' theorem, 89–91

Compatibility, 19
Conditional probability, 47
Confirmation, degree of, 50

Entrenchment, 32
Estimator, 77

Families of predicates, 48
Finite probability space, 42

Generalization principle, 14–15
Grue, 27–28, 30

Induction, justification of, 9–10

Likelihood, 67–68

Maximum likelihood, principle of, 63
Measure function, 41

Objectivity, criterion of, 8–9

Partition, 64–65
Positive confirmation, 23
Probability function, 40
Projection, 9

Qualitative predicates, 29–32

Selective confirmation, 20
Sensitivity to evidence, 7–8
Sequential test, 70
Simple inductive problem, 4
Simple predictive problem, 4
Simple statistical inference, 66–67
Simple subsets, 41
Spinner, the, 38
Statistic, 65
Strategies, 115
Structures, 52
Success, criterion of, 5–7
Sufficient statistic, 65

Universe set, 39
Utiles, 110
Utility ordering, 109